The Ultimate
Hamilton Beach

Breakfast Sandwich Maker Cookbook

Creative Breakfast Recipes to Help You Easily Make Healthy & Tasty
Hamburgers and Sandwiches in Minutes for Whole Family

Deborah Rinehart

Table of Contents

1   Introduction

2   Fundamentals of Hamilton Beach Breakfast Sandwich Maker

9   Chapter 1 Normal Breakfast Sandwiches and Omelets

18   Chapter 2 Red Meat Breakfast Sandwiches and Burgers

28   Chapter 3 Eggs Breakfast Sandwich Recipes

38   Chapter 4 Fish and Seafood Recipes

47   Chapter 5 Poultry Breakfast Sandwiches and Burgers

58   Chapter 6 Vegetarian Breakfast Recipes

67   Chapter 7 Fruit Breakfast Sandwich Recipes

77   Chapter 8 Snacks and Desserts Sandwich

87   Chapter 9 Keto Sandwich Recipes

99   Conclusion

100   Appendix 1 Measurement Conversion Chart

101   Appendix 2 Recipes Index

Introduction

Are you tired of spending your time or fortune on breakfast sandwiches from fast food chains? Do you want to enjoy a hot, fresh, and customized breakfast sandwich right in the comfort of your own home? Look no further than the Hamilton Beach Breakfast Sandwich Maker, the innovative kitchen appliance that allows you to create your own delicious breakfast sandwiches or more in just minutes.

In this book, we will explore the many ways that you can use the Hamilton Beach Breakfast Sandwich Maker to make a wide variety of breakfast sandwiches, from classic egg and cheese to more adventurous combinations like avocado and bacon or ham and pineapple. With easy-to-follow instructions and mouth-watering recipes, you'll be able to create the perfect breakfast sandwich every time.

Whether you're a busy professional who needs a quick and easy breakfast on the go, a student looking for a satisfying start to your day, or a busy parent trying to feed a hungry family, the Hamilton Beach Breakfast Sandwich Maker is the perfect solution. So why wait? Dive into this book and start creating your own delicious breakfast sandwiches today!

Fundamentals of Hamilton Beach Breakfast Sandwich Maker

It is a kitchen appliance designed to make it easy to prepare breakfast sandwiches at home. It consists of a bottom plate, two rings to hold the bread and ingredients, a cooking plate, and a top cover. The user can place the bottom half of a bread or English muffin onto the bottom plate, add ingredients such as precooked meats, vegetables, and cheese, crack an egg onto the cooking plate, and place the top half of the bread on top of the egg. The cover is closed, and the sandwich is cooked for a few minutes. The resulting sandwich can be easily removed by lifting the rings with a handle. The Hamilton Beach Breakfast Sandwich Maker is compact, easy to use, and can be a convenient appliance for anyone who enjoys making breakfast sandwiches at home.

Benefits of Using It

The Hamilton Beach Sandwich Maker is a versatile kitchen appliance that provides several benefits to its users. One of the greatest benefits of using this appliance is the convenience it offers. With this appliance, users can quickly and easily prepare breakfast sandwiches at home, saving time and effort compared to making sandwiches from scratch.

In addition to convenience, the Hamilton Beach Breakfast Sandwich Maker offers users the ability to customize their breakfast sandwiches with their preferred ingredients. This feature is particularly appealing to people who have dietary restrictions or prefer certain flavors. With this appliance, users can add a variety of ingredients, including meats, vegetables, cheese, and more, to create a breakfast sandwich that meets their specific needs and preferences.

Another advantage of using the Hamilton Beach Breakfast Sandwich Maker is that it allows users to make healthier choices. By preparing breakfast sandwiches at home, users have more control over the ingredients they use, enabling them to make healthier choices. This is particularly beneficial for people who are trying to maintain a healthy diet or have specific dietary needs.

It is also easy to clean, making it a great option for busy individuals who wanna enjoy a homemade breakfast without spending too much time cleaning up. The cooking plates and rings are removable and can be cleaned in the dishwasher or by hand, which makes cleaning up after breakfast a breeze.

In addition to being convenient, customizable, and easy to clean, the Hamilton Beach Breakfast Sandwich Maker is also a cost-effective option for people who enjoy breakfast sandwiches. Making breakfast sandwiches at home with this appliance is more affordable than buying sandwiches from a restaurant or fast-food chain, which can save users a significant amount of money over time.

Lastly, the Hamilton Beach Breakfast Sandwich Maker is versatile and can be used to make a variety of sandwiches, including muffins, bagels, biscuits, and more. This feature makes it a great addition to any kitchen, as it can be used to prepare a wide range of breakfast options.

Step-By-Step Using It

Lift the cover to remove the ring assembly of the Hamilton beach breakfast sandwich maker. To ensure the cleanliness of the removable ring assembly, it is recommended to wash it either in your dishwasher or with hot, soapy water. After washing, make sure to rinse it thoroughly and dry it properly. The top and bottom heating plates should also be wiped clean with a damp cloth that has been soaked in soapy water. To remove any remaining soap residue, use another damp cloth and dry the plates thoroughly. For optimal performance, it is advised to either spray the rings with non-stick cooking spray or brush them with vegetable oil. To ensure proper and secure use of the Hamilton Beach Breakfast Sandwich Maker, please follow these extensive instructions:

To ensure your safety, always use an oven mitt to protect your hand when opening the cover, as hot surfaces and escaping steam can cause burns. Additionally, before using the appliance, make sure to plug the cord into a wall socket. Once plugged in, you should see the red POWER light glow, indicating that the unit is receiving power.

To ensure your breakfast sandwich comes out perfectly, it's recommended to lightly spray the rings with non-stick cooking spray before each use. This will help to prevent food from sticking to the rings and make clean-up easier. To prepare the sandwich, let the unit preheat with the cover closed, and the cooking plate rotated in between the rings. Once the unit is heated to the correct temperature, the green PREHEAT light will come on and cycle on and off during cooking. Note that this light is not an indicator of when the sandwich is ready; instead, the red POWER light will stay on.

When preparing your breakfast sandwich, use the handles to lift the cover, top ring, and cooking plate. Then, place the bottom half of the bread (such as a muffin, small bagel, or bread) onto the bottom plate. Add ingredients such as precooked meats, vegetables, and cheese to the bread, being careful not to overfill the breakfast sandwich maker, as overfilling can cause food to spill over the rings and get stuck in the hinges.

Once the sandwich is loaded, move the top ring and cooking plate down. Ensure the cooking plate is firmly rotated to the back of the ring as far as it will go to prevent eggs from leaking out. Crack an egg onto the cooking plate and pierce the yolk with a toothpick or fork. You can use a whole large egg, egg white, or a scrambled egg. Top the egg with the other half of the bread, close the cover, and cook the sandwich for 4 to 5 minutes. Note that you should not push the lid all the way down when loaded with ingredients or when using a jumbo egg, as the lid may rise as the scrambled egg cooks.

When the sandwich is finished cooking, rotate the cooking plate handle clockwise until it stops. Using an oven mitt, lift the ring assembly and cover it by holding the bottom handle open. Some sandwiches may be easier to remove if the rings are lifted individually. Finally, always wait 2 minutes between cooking sandwiches to ensure that the breakfast sandwich maker is heated to the correct temperature.

Tips for Using Accessories

It is a popular kitchen appliance that allows you to quickly and easily make delicious breakfast sandwiches at home. The sandwich maker typically comes with several parts and accessories that work together to create a perfectly cooked sandwich.

Cooking plate

One of the main components of the sandwich maker is the cooking plate. This is where the egg, cheese, and other ingredients are placed in cooking. The cooking plate is typically made of a non-stick material, which helps to prevent sticking and makes clean-up a breeze.

Egg Rings

In addition to the cooking plate, the sandwich maker also comes with removable egg rings. These rings fit onto the cooking plate and are used to hold the egg in place while it cooks. The rings can be adjusted to accommodate different sizes of eggs, allowing you to create the perfect sandwich every time.

Cover

The cover of the sandwich maker is another important component. This is the top piece of the sandwich maker and is used to cover the cooking plate while the sandwich is cooking. The cover typically features a handle that stays cool to the touch, making it easy to open and close the sandwich maker without burning your fingers.

Preheat Light

Another key feature of the Hamilton Beach Breakfast Sandwich Maker is the preheat light. This is a small light on the front of the sandwich maker that illuminates when the unit is preheated and ready to use. This helps to ensure that your sandwich is cooked evenly and to perfection every time.

Power Cord:

The sandwich maker also comes with a power cord that plugs into an electrical outlet and provides power to the unit. And, of course, no kitchen appliance would be complete without an instruction manual. The Hamilton Beach Breakfast Sandwich Maker typically comes with an instruction manual that provides super-detailed instructions on how to use the sandwich maker, as well as recipes for making different types of breakfast sandwiches.

Cleaning and Caring

It is important to carefully follow these guidelines to ensure the safe use of the product and prevent any potential risk of electrical shock or damage:

Disconnect the power source before cleaning: Before attempting to clean the unit, it is crucial to disconnect it from the power source. Failure to do so could result in an electrical shock hazard. Ensure that all electrical connections are unplugged and the unit is completely disconnected from the power source before cleaning any part of the appliance.

Wait for the unit to cool down: After using the unit, always unplug it and allow it to cool down before attempting to clean it. Hot surfaces could cause injury or damage to the product if cleaning is attempted immediately after use.

Be cautious when removing the ring assembly: To remove the ring assembly for cleaning, hold the bottom handle to open it and then lift it straight up. However, it is essential to be careful not to damage any part

of the unit while doing so. Ensure that all components are removed safely and without causing any harm to the product.

Avoid using abrasive cleaners: It is important not to use steel wool, scouring pads, or abrasive cleaners on any part of the unit. These can scratch and damage the surfaces and affect the functioning of the product. Also, never use sharp or pointed objects for cleaning, as these could cause permanent damage to the appliance.

Be cautious while washing in a dishwasher: When washing the unit in the dishwasher, avoid using the high-temperature sanitizing setting. The "SANI" cycle temperatures could be too high and cause damage to the product. Ensure that you use the recommended temperature settings for washing the unit.

Use a lightly damp, soapy cloth to clean the heating plates: To clean the top and bottom heating plates, use a damp, soapy cloth. Ensure that any soap residue is removed with a damp cloth and the unit is dried thoroughly before using it again.

Be careful while replacing the ring assembly: When replacing the ring assembly, align the tabs on the ring assembly with the openings on the hinge of the base, and lower it carefully into place. Ensure that all components are securely attached without any damage.

Wipe the outside of the unit: Finally, wipe the outside of the unit with a lightly damp, soapy cloth to remove any dirt or grime. Ensure that the unit is dried thoroughly before using it again to avoid any potential damage.

Frequently Asked Questions & Notes

Q: How long does it take to cook a breakfast sandwich in the Hamilton Beach Breakfast Sandwich Maker?
A: Typically, it takes about 4 to 5 minutes to cook a breakfast sandwich in the Hamilton Beach Breakfast Sandwich Maker. However, the exact cooking time may vary depending on the type of bread and ingredients you use, as well as your personal preference for the level of doneness of the egg. To get the best results when cooking with the Breakfast Sandwich Maker, it's important to follow the manufacturer's instructions carefully. Make sure to preheat the appliance with the cover closed and the cooking plate rotated in between the rings. Once the green PREHEAT light comes on, you can start assembling your sandwich and cooking it with the cover closed.

Q: Can I use regular bread in the Breakfast Sandwich Maker?
A: If you're wondering whether you can use regular bread in the Hamilton Beach Breakfast Sandwich Maker, the answer is yes, you certainly can! However, there are some things to keep in mind to ensure that your sandwich turns out perfectly. First, it's important to slice the bread thinly so that it fits easily into the rings of the Breakfast Sandwich Maker. Thick slices of bread may not fit properly and could cause the rings to become stuck or damaged.

Q: Can I make more than one sandwich at a time in the Breakfast Sandwich Maker?
A: If you're wondering whether the Hamilton Beach Breakfast Sandwich Maker can make more than one sandwich at a time, the answer is no; it is designed to make only one sandwich at a time. This is because the rings and cooking plate are specifically sized to hold the ingredients for a single sandwich, and using more ingredients could result in the sandwich overflowing or not cooking evenly.

Q: How do I clean the Breakfast Sandwich Maker?
A: When you're finished making breakfast sandwiches with your

Hamilton Beach Breakfast Sandwich Maker, it's important to clean it thoroughly to ensure that it stays in good condition and is ready for your next use. To do this, the first step is to unplug the unit and allow it to cool down before cleaning. This will help to prevent any accidents and also ensure that the appliance is safe to handle. Once your unit has cooled down, you can start cleaning it by removing the rings and cooking plate. These parts can be washed in warm, soapy water or in the dishwasher for easy and convenient cleaning. It's important to make sure that the rings and cooking plate are completely clean and free of any food particles or residue, as this can affect the flavor, texture, and quality of your sandwiches.

Q: Can I cook raw meat in the Breakfast Sandwich Maker?
A: When it comes to using your Hamilton Beach Breakfast Sandwich Maker to prepare tasty breakfast sandwiches, it's important to be mindful of the types of ingredients you use. While the appliance can be a convenient way to cook a variety of breakfast items, it's not recommended to cook raw meat in the Breakfast Sandwich Maker. This is because cooking raw meat in the appliance can pose a food safety risk, as the sandwich maker may not heat the meat to the appropriate temperature to kill harmful bacteria. Instead, it's recommended to use precooked meats such as ham, bacon, or sausage, which can be safely heated in the sandwich maker.

Q: Can I make vegetarian or vegan sandwiches in the Breakfast Sandwich Maker?
A: One of the great things about the Hamilton Beach Breakfast Sandwich Maker is its versatility in terms of the types of sandwiches you can make. Whether you're a vegetarian or vegan, you can easily create delicious and satisfying breakfast sandwiches using plant-based proteins, tofu, or vegetables.
For vegetarians, plant-based meats such as veggie sausage or bacon can be used as a tasty substitute for traditional meat. These products can be found in many grocery stores and offer a similar taste and texture to their meat-based counterparts. Tofu is another great option for vegetarians, as it can be scrambled and used as a filling for your breakfast sandwich.

Q: Can I use frozen bread or ingredients in the Breakfast Sandwich Maker?
A: While it may be tempting to use frozen bread or other ingredients in a rush, it is not recommended to do so, as this can affect the cooking process and lead to unevenly cooked sandwiches. When ingredients are frozen, they take longer to cook, which can result in overcooking the sandwich or even burning it. In addition, using frozen bread can cause the sandwich to become soggy, as the moisture from the frozen bread can be released during the cooking process.
To avoid these issues, it is recommended to thaw ingredients before using them in the Breakfast Sandwich Maker. This can be done by placing the ingredients in your refrigerator overnight or using a microwave to defrost them. Thawing the ingredients before use will help to ensure that they cook evenly and that the sandwich has the desired texture and taste.

Q: Can I use the Breakfast Sandwich Maker to cook other types of sandwiches?
A: The Hamilton Beach Breakfast Sandwich Maker can be a versatile kitchen appliance, as it is not limited to making just breakfast sandwiches. You can use it to make a variety of sandwiches by changing the ingredients to suit your taste. For example, you can make a grilled cheese sandwich by replacing the egg and meat with cheese and bread. You can also make a tuna melt sandwich by using canned tuna, mayonnaise, and cheese. Another option is to make a chicken sandwich by using grilled or baked chicken breast, cheese, and other toppings. The possibilities are endless, and you can get creative with your sandwich-making using the Breakfast Sandwich Maker.

Troubleshooting

Low, Poor, Or Slow Heating

To ensure that your breakfast sandwich is cooked to perfection, it's important to preheat the sandwich maker properly. This involves waiting until the green PREHEAT light illuminates, which typically takes around 5 to 7 minutes. It's important to note that the light simply indicates that the unit has reached the correct temperature and doesn't necessarily mean that the sandwich is ready to be cooked. To ensure the best results, it's recommended that you wait an additional 2 minutes after the PREHEAT light comes on before making your sandwich.

When using the breakfast sandwich maker, it's important to give the unit enough time to heat up between sandwiches. Ideally, you should wait at least 2 minutes before making your next sandwich. This will ensure that the cooking plate is properly heated and your sandwich cooks evenly.

If you find that your breakfast sandwich maker is overfilled, it's likely that you're using too many ingredients. To avoid this, try reducing the amount of filling that you use in your sandwich. This will ensure that the ingredients cook evenly and that your sandwich doesn't overflow.

To preheat the breakfast sandwich maker properly, it's important to ensure that the cover is closed and that the rings and cooking plate are in place. This will help to spread the heat evenly and ensure that your sandwich cooks properly. It's also important to make sure that the cooking plate is rotated securely to the back of the ring as far as it will go. This will prevent any leaks from the egg or other ingredients.

To ensure that your breakfast sandwich maker works properly, it's important to follow the manufacturer's instructions carefully. This includes making sure that the cooking plate is rotated securely to the back of the ring and that the cover is closed when preheating the unit. These steps will help to ensure that your sandwich cooks evenly and that you get the best possible results.

Egg Undercooked, bread not done

If you're using extra-large eggs, frozen ingredients, or ingredients that are very cold, this may increase the overall cooking time of your sandwich. To compensate for this, you may need to add additional cooking time to ensure that your sandwich is fully cooked. If you find that your egg is overcooked, this may be a sign that you're cooking it for too long. It's important to monitor your sandwich carefully to ensure that it's cooked to your liking.

When using the breakfast sandwich maker, it's important to keep in mind that the cooking time can vary depending on various factors. For example, if you're using small eggs, scrambled eggs, or egg whites, the cooking time may be different than if you're using a whole egg. To ensure that your sandwich is cooked properly, it's important to reduce the cooking time for future recipes based on these variables. In general, the cooking time for a breakfast sandwich is around 5 minutes, but you may need to adjust this based on your individual preferences and the ingredients that you're using.

Ingredients stick to rings or non-stick cooking plates.

To ensure that your breakfast sandwich maker stays in good condition and continues to function properly, it's important to take care when cleaning it. If you find that there are baked-on ingredients stuck to the cooking surface, it's best to use a plastic or wooden utensil to loosen them. This will help to prevent any damage to the non-stick surface. Additionally, it's a good idea to lightly spray the cooking surface with non-stick cooking spray before preheating for the next use. This will help to prevent any sticking and ensure that your sandwich comes out perfectly every time.

If you find that your breakfast sandwich maker is leaking eggs out of the rings, this may be a sign that the unit is overfilled. To avoid this, it's important to only use large eggs and to reduce the amount or size of ingredients that you're using. It's also important not to press down on the cover, as this can cause the eggs to leak out. By following these special tips, you can ensure that your breakfast sandwich maker functions properly and that your sandwiches turn out perfectly every time.

When using the breakfast sandwich maker, it's important to make sure that the cooking plate is in the correct position to prevent any leaking of eggs. This involves rotating the cooking plate securely to the back of the ring as far as it will go. If you find that your sandwich maker is leaking eggs, it's possible that the cooking plate wasn't in the correct position. By taking care to ensure that the cooking plate is securely in place, you can prevent any leaks and ensure that your breakfast sandwich turns out perfectly.

If you've had trouble with thin purchased egg whites leaking out of your breakfast sandwich maker, it may be worth trying a different brand or using fresh egg whites instead. Different brands of egg whites can have different consistencies and may work better or worse in your sandwich maker. Additionally, using fresh egg whites can ensure that they have the right consistency and are less likely to leak out.

Cover Rises When Cooking My Sandwich

When using the breakfast sandwich maker to cook scrambled eggs, it's important to keep in mind that the air whisked into a large scrambled egg can cause the cover to rise while the egg is cooking. This can be alarming, but it's important not to press down on the cover, as this can cause the egg to spill out and potentially cause burns or other injuries. Instead, simply wait for the egg to finish cooking and for the cover to settle back down before removing your sandwich from the maker.

If you find that your bread is coming out too brown when using the breakfast sandwich maker, it may be due to higher fat content and sugars in the bread. These can cause the bread to darken more quickly than other types of bread. To avoid this, you may want to try cooking your egg for several minutes without the bread and cover it down. This will allow the egg to cook fully without the bread being exposed to heat for too long. Once the egg is cooked, you can add the bread and finish cooking your sandwich to perfection.

Chapter 1 Normal Breakfast Sandwiches and Omelets

10 Classic Bacon, Lettuce, and Tomato Sandwich

10 Cheese Egg Sandwich

10 Herbed Cheese Spinach Sandwiches

11 Spicy Mushroom Kale Sandwich

11 Breakfast Frittata Sandwich

12 Cheese Ham Biscuit Sandwiches

12 Sausage and Waffle Sandwich

12 Bacon and Egg Sandwich

13 Cheddar Ham Muffin

13 Parmesan Spinach Sandwich

13 Herbed Onion and Egg Cheese Muffins

14 Cream Cheese Egg Sandwich

14 Cheese Sausage Egg Muffin Sandwich

14 Cheddar Sausage Biscuit Sandwich

15 Egg and Ham Whole-Grain Sandwich

15 Cheesy Egg, Avocado, and Bacon Sandwich

15 Maple Bacon French Toast Breakfast Sandwich

16 Crispy Chicken Biscuits

16 Mexican Beans & Fried Egg Sandwich

17 Mayo Avocado and Vegetables Sandwich

17 Beef Cheeseburger

Classic Bacon, Lettuce, and Tomato Sandwich

Prep Time: 15 minutes | Cook Time: 5 minutes | Serves: 1

Ingredients:

2 slices white bread, cut in 4-inch circle
3 bacon slices, cooked
2 thin tomato slices

1 leaf Romaine lettuce, torn in half
2 teaspoons mayonnaise

Preparation:

1. Preheat the Breakfast Sandwich Maker until the green PREHEAT light comes on. Lift cover, top ring, and cooking plate. 2. Place one half of the bread in the bottom ring of the sandwich maker. 3. Spread the mayonnaise on top and layer the lettuce and tomato. 4. Lower the cooking plate and top ring, then place the bacon in the cooking plate and place the other slice of the bread on top. 5. Close the cover and cook for 5 minutes. Rotate the cooking plate handle clockwise until it stops. 6. Then lift the cover and rings and carefully remove the sandwich with plastic spatula. 7. Serve.

Serving Suggestion: Serve the sandwich with crispy bacon and your favorite sauce on the side.

Variation Tip: Add some additional ground black pepper to the filling.

Nutritional Information Per Serving: Calories 267 | Fat 12g |Sodium 165mg | Carbs 39g | Fiber 1.4g | Sugar 22g | Protein 3.3g

Cheese Egg Sandwich

Prep Time: 15 minutes | Cook Time: 5 minutes | Serves: 1

Ingredients:

1 English Muffin
1 large egg, beaten

1 cheese slice,
Butter, or olive oil

Preparation:

1. Preheat the Breakfast Sandwich Maker until the green PREHEAT light comes on. Lift cover, top ring, and cooking plate. 2. Place the lower half of the muffin in the bottom ring of the sandwich maker. 3. Brush the top of the muffin half with butter. 4. Lower cooking plate and top ring. Add egg to cooking plate. Pierce yolk with a fork or toothpick. 5. Top the egg with cheese slice and top with the other half of the muffin. 6. Close the cover and cook for 5 minutes. Rotate the cooking plate handle clockwise until it stops. Then lift the cover and rings and carefully remove the sandwich with plastic spatula. 7. Serve.

Serving Suggestion: Serve the sandwich with coleslaw and your favorite sauce on the side.

Variation Tip: Add some additional dried herbs to the filling.

Nutritional Information Per Serving: Calories 273 | Fat 22g |Sodium 517mg | Carbs 3.3g | Fiber 0.2g | Sugar 1.4g | Protein 16.1g

Herbed Cheese Spinach Sandwiches

Prep Time: 15 minutes | Cook Time: 5 minutes | Serves: 2

Ingredients:

2 buns, sliced
4 teaspoons olive oil
1 tablespoon snipped fresh rosemary
4 eggs, beaten
2 cups fresh baby spinach leaves

1 tomato, cut into 8 thin slices
4 tablespoons low-fat feta cheese
⅛ teaspoon kosher salt
Freshly ground black pepper.

Preparation:

1. In a medium bowl, beat the eggs with black pepper and salt. 2. Preheat the Breakfast Sandwich Maker until the green PREHEAT light comes on. Lift cover, top ring, and cooking plate. 3. Place half of a bun in the bottom ring of the sandwich maker. 4. Spread half of the toppings on top except the egg mixture. 5. Lower cooking plate and top ring. Pour half of the egg into cooking plate. 6. Top with the other top half of the bun. 7. Close the cover and cook for 5 minutes. Rotate the cooking plate handle clockwise until it stops. Then lift the cover and rings and carefully remove the sandwich with plastic spatula. 8. Repeat the process for the remaining ingredients. 9. Serve.

Serving Suggestion: Serve the sandwich with your favorite sauce on the side.

Variation Tip: You can add a layer of your favorite sauce to the filling as well.

Nutritional Information Per Serving: Calories 237 | Fat 19g |Sodium 518mg | Carbs 7g | Fiber 1.5g | Sugar 3.4g | Protein 12g

Spicy Mushroom Kale Sandwich

Prep time: 15 minutes | Cook Time: 28 minutes | Serves: 4

Ingredients:

Marinated mushrooms

½ shallot, sliced

1 sprig thyme

4 ounces King trumpet mushrooms, sliced

¼ cup olive oil

¼ cup white wine vinegar

1½ teaspoons kosher salt

Sautéed kale

2 tablespoons olive oil

1 medium onion, chopped

2 garlic cloves, chopped

2 large bunches of kale, chopped

½ teaspoon crushed red pepper flakes

Salt and black pepper, to taste

Mushroom mayonnaise

¼ cup dried mushrooms

½ shallot, chopped

½ cup mayonnaise

1 tablespoon fresh lemon juice

1 teaspoon rosemary, chopped

Salt and black pepper, to taste

Assembly

2 tablespoons olive oil

1 tablespoon unsalted butter

4 large eggs

4 English muffins, split

4 slices Swiss cheese

4 teaspoons green chile hot sauce

Preparation:

1. In a bowl, mix all the marinated mushroom ingredients. Cover and refrigerate for 1 hour at least. 2. Add the marinated mushrooms to the pan and sauté for 5 minutes, then set aside. 3. Add all the sautéed kale ingredients to the pan and cook for 3 minutes, then transfer to a plate. 4. Soak the dried mushrooms in a bowl of water for 10 minutes, then drain and chop. 5. Mix the rehydrated mushrooms in a bowl with the rest of the mushroom mayonnaise ingredients. 6. Preheat the Breakfast Sandwich Maker until the green PREHEAT light comes on. Lift cover, top ring, and cooking plate. 7. Place half of the English muffin, cut-side up, in the bottom ring of the sandwich maker. 8. Top with ¼ of the mushroom mayonnaise, marinated mushrooms and kale. 9. Beat the eggs in a small bowl. 10. Lower cooking plate and top ring. Add egg to cooking plate. 11. Top with one slice of cheese and another half of the muffin, then brush it with butter. 12. Close the cover and cook for 5 minutes. Rotate the cooking plate handle clockwise until it stops. Then lift the cover and rings and carefully remove the sandwich with plastic spatula. 13. Repeat the same steps with the remaining muffins and ingredients. 14. Serve.

Serving Suggestion: Serve the sandwich with a broccoli salad on the side.

Variation Tip: Add a layer of spicy mayo and pickled veggies for a change of taste.

Nutritional Information Per Serving: Calories 297 | Fat 15g |Sodium 548mg | Carbs 5g | Fiber 4g | Sugar 1g | Protein 19g

Breakfast Frittata Sandwich

Prep time: 15 minutes | Cook Time: 25 minutes | Serves: 4

Ingredients:

½ cup fresh parsley leaves, chopped

2 tablespoons capers

2 tablespoons red onion, chopped

½ teaspoons crushed red pepper flakes

¼ cup olive oil

2 tablespoons red wine vinegar

½ teaspoons sugar

Salt and black pepper, to taste

8 bread slices, cut into 4 inches round

8 eggs

4 cups kale leaves

Preparation:

1. In a skillet over medium heat, sauté red onion with oil, red pepper flakes, black pepper, capers, sugar, salt and vinegar for 5 minutes. 2. Preheat the Breakfast Sandwich Maker until the green PREHEAT light comes on. Lift cover, top ring, and cooking plate. 3. Place one bread slice inside the bottom ring of the sandwich maker. 4. In a small bowl, beat the eggs with onion mixture, kale leaves, salt and black pepper. 5. Lower cooking plate and top ring. Add ¼ of the egg mixture to cooking plate. 6. Place another bread slice on top. 7. Close the cover and cook for 5 minutes. Rotate the cooking plate handle clockwise until it stops. Then lift the cover and rings and carefully remove the sandwich with plastic spatula. 8. Repeat the process for the remaining ingredients. 9. Serve.

Serving Suggestion: Serve the sandwich with crispy sweet potato fries on the side.

Variation Tip: Add a layer of pickled onions for a change of taste.

Nutritional Information Per Serving: Calories 322 | Fat 12g |Sodium 202mg | Carbs 24.6g | Fiber 4g | Sugar 8g | Protein 17.3g

Cheese Ham Biscuit Sandwiches

Prep time: 15 minutes | Cook Time: 40 minutes | Serves: 8

Ingredients:

8 biscuits, cut in half
8 teaspoons butter
8 tablespoons black mission fig jam

12 ounces sliced ham
12 tablespoons grated sharp cheddar cheese
½ cup Heirloom grits

Preparation:

1. Preheat the Breakfast Sandwich Maker until the green PREHEAT light comes on. Lift cover, top ring, and cooking plate. 2. Place half of the biscuit, cut-side up, in the bottom ring of the sandwich maker. 3. Spread the 1 teaspoon butter and 1 tablespoon jam on top of the biscuit half. 4. Lower cooking plate and top ring. Add ⅛ of the ham, grits and cheese. 5. Top with the other top half of the biscuit. 6. Close the cover and cook for 5 minutes. Rotate the cooking plate handle clockwise until it stops. Then lift the cover and rings and carefully remove the sandwich with plastic spatula. 7. Repeat the process for the remaining ingredients. 8. Serve.

Serving Suggestion: Serve the sandwich with crispy fries on the side.

Variation Tip: Add a layer of pickled veggies for a change of taste.

Nutritional Information Per Serving: Calories 312 | Fat 25g |Sodium 132mg | Carbs 4g | Fiber 3.9g | Sugar 3g | Protein 18.9g

Sausage and Waffle Sandwich

Prep Time: 15 minutes | Cook Time: 5 minutes | Serves: 1

Ingredients:

2 round frozen waffles
1 pork sausage patty, cooked

1 large egg, beaten
1 teaspoon maple syrup

Preparation:

1. Preheat the Breakfast Sandwich Maker until the green PREHEAT light comes on. Lift cover, top ring, and cooking plate. 2. Place one of the waffle in the bottom ring of the sandwich maker and top it with patty. 3. Lower cooking plate and top ring. Crack an egg to cooking plate and drizzle with maple syrup. 4. Top with the other top half of the waffle. 5. Close the cover and cook for 5 minutes. Rotate the cooking plate handle clockwise until it stops. Then lift the cover and rings and carefully remove the sandwich with plastic spatula. 6. Serve.

Serving Suggestion: Serve the sandwich with your favorite sauce on the side.

Variation Tip: You can add a lettuce leave to the filling as well.

Nutritional Information Per Serving: Calories 284 | Fat 7.9g |Sodium 704mg | Carbs 38.1g | Fiber 1.9g | Sugar 1.9g | Protein 14.8g

Bacon and Egg Sandwich

Prep time: 15 minutes | Cook Time: 15 minutes | Serves: 2

Ingredients:

4 slices thick-cut bacon
4 ¾-inch-thick sourdough bread slices, cut into 4-inch round
4 large eggs
Salt and black pepper, to taste

2 tablespoons unsalted butter
4 slices cheddar
4 teaspoons Hot sauce, for serving

Preparation:

1. In a skillet over medium heat, sauté the bacon for 5 minutes on each side until golden brown. 2. Preheat the Breakfast Sandwich Maker until the green PREHEAT light comes on. Lift cover, top ring, and cooking plate. 3. Place a bread slice, inside the bottom ring of the sandwich maker. 4. Brush the top of the bread with butter and place 2 bacon slices on top. 5. In a small bowl, beat the egg with black pepper and salt. 6. Lower cooking plate and top ring. Pour the egg into cooking plate. 7. Top with a cheddar cheese slice and the other bread slice. 8. Close the cover and cook for 5 minutes. Rotate the cooking plate handle clockwise until it stops. Then lift the cover and rings and carefully remove the sandwich with plastic spatula. 9. Repeat the same step with the remaining ingredients. 10. Serve with the hot sauce.

Serving Suggestion: Serve the sandwich with a cauliflower bacon salad on the side.

Variation Tip: Enjoy sautéed veggies on the side for a change of taste.

Nutritional Information Per Serving: Calories 311 | Fat 12.5g |Sodium 595mg | Carbs 3g | Fiber 12g | Sugar 12g | Protein 17g

Cheddar Ham Muffin

Prep Time: 15 minutes | Cook Time: 5 minutes | Serves: 1

Ingredients:

1 toasted English muffin, sliced
2 slices deli ham
1 slice cheddar cheese
1 large egg, beaten

Preparation:

1. Preheat the Breakfast Sandwich Maker until the green PREHEAT light comes on. Lift cover, top ring, and cooking plate. 2. Place half of the muffin in the bottom ring of the sandwich maker and top with the ham slices. 3. Lower cooking plate and top ring. Add egg to cooking plate. 4. Place the cheese slice and top with half of the bun. 5. Close the cover and cook for 5 minutes. Rotate the cooking plate handle clockwise until it stops. Then lift the cover and rings and carefully remove the sandwich with plastic spatula. 6. Serve.

Serving Suggestion: Serve the sandwich with crispy bacon and your favorite sauce on the side.

Variation Tip: Add some additional ground black pepper to the filling.

Nutritional Information Per Serving: Calories 307 | Fat 8.6g |Sodium 510mg | Carbs 22.2g | Fiber 1.4g | Sugar 13g | Protein 33.6g

Parmesan Spinach Sandwich

Prep Time: 15 minutes | Cook Time: 5 minutes | Serves: 1

Ingredients:

1 toasted English muffin, sliced
½ cup baby spinach leaves
2 large egg whites
1 tablespoon grated parmesan cheese
1 garlic clove, minced

Preparation:

1. Preheat the Breakfast Sandwich Maker until the green PREHEAT light comes on. Lift cover, top ring, and cooking plate. 2. Place half of the English muffin, cut-side up, inside the bottom ring of the sandwich maker. 3. Spread the baby spinach leaves on top of the English muffin. 4. In a small bowl, beat the egg whites, garlic and parmesan cheese. 5. Lower cooking plate and top ring. Then pour the egg mixture to the cooking plate. 6. Top with the other half of the muffin. 7. Close the cover and cook for 5 minutes. Rotate the cooking plate handle clockwise until it stops. Then lift the cover and rings and carefully remove the sandwich with plastic spatula. 8. Serve.

Serving Suggestion: Serve the sandwich with crispy bacon and your favorite sauce on the side.

Variation Tip: You can add a lettuce leave to the filling as well.

Nutritional Information Per Serving: Calories 282 | Fat 15g |Sodium 526mg | Carbs 20g | Fiber 0.6g | Sugar 3.3g | Protein 16g

Herbed Onion and Egg Cheese Muffins

Prep time: 15 minutes | Cook Time: 10 minutes | Serves: 2

Ingredients:

1 red onion, peeled, separated into rings
1 teaspoon soy sauce
½ teaspoons garlic powder
2 tablespoons olive oil
Salt, to taste
¼ cup soft herbs, chopped
2 tablespoons green hot sauce
1 tablespoon unsalted butter
4 large eggs, beaten
2 whole-grain English muffins, toasted
2 ounces sharp cheddar cheese, sliced

Preparation:

1. In a bowl, toss the onion with soy sauce, garlic powder, salt, herbs, olive oil, and sauce. 2. Preheat the Breakfast Sandwich Maker until the green PREHEAT light comes on. Lift cover, top ring, and cooking plate. 3. Place half of the English muffin, cut-side up, inside the bottom ring of the sandwich maker. 4. Brush the top with butter and spread ½ of the onion mixture. 5. Lower cooking plate and top ring. Pour ½ of the egg into the cooking plate. 6. Add the cheese and top with the other half of the muffin. Brush it with butter. 7. Close the cover and cook for 5 minutes. Rotate the cooking plate handle clockwise until it stops. Then lift the cover and rings and carefully remove the sandwich with plastic spatula. 8. Repeat the process for the remaining ingredients. 9. Serve.

Serving Suggestion: Serve the sandwich with crispy fries on the side.

Variation Tip: Add a layer of pickled veggies for a change of taste.

Nutritional Information Per Serving: Calories 404 | Fat 13g |Sodium 216mg | Carbs 7g | Fiber 3g | Sugar 4g | Protein 31g

Cream Cheese Egg Sandwich

Prep time: 15 minutes | Cook Time: 10 minutes | Serves: 2

Ingredients:

Scrambled eggs
4 large eggs
1 small pinch of cayenne pepper
Kosher salt, to taste

2 tablespoons unsalted butter
3 tablespoons cream cheese

Assembly
2 American cheese slices

4 thick potato bread slices, cut into 4 inches' round

Preparation:

1. In a bowl, beat the egg with cream cheese, butter, cayenne pepper and salt. 2. Preheat the Breakfast Sandwich Maker until the green PREHEAT light comes on. Lift cover, top ring, and cooking plate. 3. Place one bread slice, inside the bottom ring of the sandwich maker. 4. Lower cooking plate and top ring. Pour ½ the egg into the cooking plate. 5. Top with one cheese slice and the other bread slice. 6. Close the cover and cook for 5 minutes. Rotate the cooking plate handle clockwise until it stops. Then lift the cover and rings and carefully remove the sandwich with plastic spatula. 7. Repeat the same steps with the remaining ingredients. 8. Serve.

Serving Suggestion: Serve the sandwich with a broccoli salad on the side.

Variation Tip: Add a layer of spicy mayo and pickled veggies for a change of taste.

Nutritional Information Per Serving: Calories 348 | Fat 12g |Sodium 710mg | Carbs 4g | Fiber 5g | Sugar 3g | Protein 31g

Cheese Sausage Egg Muffin Sandwich

Prep time: 15 minutes | Cook Time: 5 minutes | Serves: 1

Ingredients:

1 tablespoon unsalted butter
1 English muffin, split
1 breakfast sausage patty, cooked
2 slices American cheese

2 large eggs, beaten
Salt and black pepper, to taste
1 handful of fresh chives, chopped
Hot sauce and honey, for serving

Preparation:

1. In a bowl, beat the eggs with salt, black pepper, chives, honey and hot sauce. 2. Preheat the Breakfast Sandwich Maker until the green PREHEAT light comes on. Lift cover, top ring, and cooking plate. 3. Place half of the English muffin, cut-side up, inside the bottom ring of the sandwich maker. Brush it with butter. 4. Top with the sausage patty. 5. Lower cooking plate and top ring. Add the egg mixture to cooking plate. 6. Top with the cheese slices and the other half of the muffin. 7. Close the cover and cook for 5 minutes. Rotate the cooking plate handle clockwise until it stops. Then lift the cover and rings and carefully remove the sandwich with plastic spatula. 8. Serve.

Serving Suggestion: Serve the sandwich with crispy carrot chips on the side.

Variation Tip: Add a layer of sliced bell peppers for a change of taste.

Nutritional Information Per Serving: Calories 375 | Fat 16g |Sodium 255mg | Carbs 4.1g | Fiber 1.2g | Sugar 5g | Protein 24.1g

Cheddar Sausage Biscuit Sandwich

Prep Time: 15 minutes | Cook Time: 5 minutes | Serves: 1

Ingredients:

1 buttermilk biscuit, sliced
1 maple pork sausage patty, cooked

1 slice cheddar cheese
1 large egg, beaten

Preparation:

1. Preheat the Breakfast Sandwich Maker until the green PREHEAT light comes on. Lift cover, top ring, and cooking plate. 2. Place half of the biscuit, cut-side up, inside the bottom ring of the sandwich maker. 3. Top with the sausage patty and the slice of cheddar cheese. 4. Lower cooking plate and top ring. Add egg to cooking plate. 5. Top with the other top half of the biscuit. 6. Close the cover and cook for 5 minutes. Rotate the cooking plate handle clockwise until it stops. Then lift the cover and rings and carefully remove the sandwich with plastic spatula. 7. Serve.

Serving Suggestion: Serve the sandwich with your favorite sauce on the side.

Variation Tip: Add some additional dried herbs to the filling.

Nutritional Information Per Serving: Calories 270 | Fat 14.6g |Sodium 394mg | Carbs 31.3g | Fiber 7.5g | Sugar 9.7g | Protein 6.4g

Egg and Ham Whole-Grain Sandwich

Prep Time: 15 minutes | Cook Time: 5 minutes | Serves: 1

Ingredients:

2 slices whole grain bread, cut in 4-inch circle
2 slices deli ham
1 slice Swiss cheese

1 large egg
2 teaspoons heavy cream
1 teaspoon chopped chives

Preparation:

1. Preheat your Hamilton Beach Breakfast Sandwich Maker. 2. Place one slice of bread in the bottom tray of the sandwich maker. 3. Arrange the slices of ham on top of the bread and top with the slice of Swiss cheese. 4. Beat together the egg, heavy cream and chives in a small bowl. 5. Slide the egg tray into place over the cheese and pour the beaten egg mixture into the tray. 6. Top the egg mixture with the remaining slice of bread. 7. Cover the top hood, and let the sandwich cook for 5 minutes. 8. When finished cooking, rotate the handle of the cooking plate clockwise until it stops. 9. Lift the hood, the rings and transfer the sandwich to a plate. 10. Serve.

Serving Suggestion: Serve the sandwich with coleslaw and your favorite sauce on the side.

Variation Tip: You can add a layer of your favorite sauce to the filling as well.

Nutritional Information Per Serving: Calories 350 | Fat 2.6g |Sodium 358mg | Carbs 64.6g | Fiber 14.4g | Sugar 3.3g | Protein 19.9g

Cheesy Egg, Avocado, and Bacon Sandwich

Prep Time: 15 minutes | Cook Time: 5 minutes | Serves: 1

Ingredients:

1 croissant, sliced
2 bacon slices, cooked
1 slice Swiss cheese

¼ avocado, pitted and sliced
1 large egg
1 tablespoon basil pesto

Preparation:

1. Preheat your Hamilton Beach Breakfast Sandwich Maker. 2. Divide the pesto between the two halves of the croissant, spreading it evenly. 3. Place half of the croissant, pesto-side up, inside the bottom tray of the sandwich maker. 4. Arrange the slices of bacon on top of the bagel and top with the slice of Swiss cheese. 5. Slide the egg tray into place and crack the egg into it. 6. Top the egg with the other top half of the croissant, pesto-side down. 7. Cover the top hood, and let the sandwich cook for 5 minutes. 8. When finished cooking, rotate the handle of the cooking plate clockwise until it stops. 9. Lift the hood, the rings and transfer the sandwich to a plate. 10. Serve.

Serving Suggestion: Serve the sandwich with your favorite sauce on the side.

Variation Tip: Add some additional ground black pepper to the filling.

Nutritional Information Per Serving: Calories 288 | Fat 6.9g |Sodium 761mg | Carbs 46g | Fiber 4g | Sugar 12g | Protein 9.6g

Maple Bacon French Toast Breakfast Sandwich

Prep Time: 15 minutes | Cook Time: 5 minutes | Serves: 2

Ingredients:

2 beaten eggs
¼ cup milk
½ teaspoon cinnamon
Filling:
4 bacon slices
2 eggs, beaten

Dash of nutmeg
2 tablespoons butter
4 slices white bread, cut in 4-inch circle

4 tablespoons maple syrup

Preparation:

1. Combine the eggs, milk, cinnamon and nutmeg in a bowl. 2. Coat each bread slice with the mixture. 3. Preheat your Hamilton Beach Breakfast Sandwich Maker. 4. Lift the top cover, ring, and cooking plate. 5. Brush one bread slice with the 1 tablespoon butter, place it in the sandwich maker and top it with ½ of the bacon strip. 6. Now lower the cooking plate and top rings then pour in ½ of the eggs on top. 7. Add the other circle of the bread on top. 8. Cover the top hood, and let the sandwich cook for 5 minutes. 9. When finished cooking, rotate the handle of the cooking plate clockwise until it stops. 10. Lift the hood, the rings and transfer the sandwich to a plate. 11. Serve.

Serving Suggestion: Serve the sandwich with crispy bacon and your favorite sauce on the side.

Variation Tip: You can add a drizzle of paprika on top of the filling as well.

Nutritional Information Per Serving: Calories 354; Fat 7.9g; Sodium 704mg; Carbs 6g; Fiber 3.6g; Sugar 6g; Protein 18g

Crispy Chicken Biscuits

Prep time: 15 minutes | Cook Time: 15 minutes | Serves: 4

Ingredients:

Chicken cutlets
1 cup buttermilk
1 tablespoon hot sauce
½ teaspoon salt

Honey butter
½ cup unsalted butter
¼ cup honey

For cooking:
Vegetable oil, for frying
2 cups Japanese breadcrumbs
Black pepper, to taste

¼ teaspoon black pepper
¼ teaspoon cayenne pepper
4 boneless chicken cutlets

½ teaspoon kosher salt

4 pies-n-thighs biscuits
Hot sauce, for serving

Preparation:

1. Mix chicken cutlets with buttermilk, cayenne pepper, black pepper, salt, and hot sauce in a suitable bowl. 2. Cover and marinate this chicken for 30 minutes at least in the refrigerator. 3. Meanwhile, mix butter with salt and honey in a bowl. 4. Remove the chicken from its marinade, coat it with honey mixture. 5. Coat the honey chicken with panko crumbs and drizzle black pepper on top. 6. Set a pan with vegetable oil for frying on medium-high heat. 7. Fry the chicken cutlets until golden brown and keep them aside. 8. Preheat your Hamilton Beach Breakfast Sandwich Maker until PREHEAT light gets green. 9. Lift the top cover, ring, and cooking plate. 10. Place half a biscuit, cut-side up, inside the bottom tray of the sandwich maker. 11. Now lower the cooking plate and top rings, then place a chicken cutlet and add breadcrumbs. 12. Place the other top half of the biscuit on top. 13. Cover the top hood, and let it cook for 5 minutes. 14. Rotate the handle of the cooking plate clockwise until it stops. 15. Lift the hood, the rings and transfer the biscuit to a plate. 16. Repeat the same steps with the remaining ingredients. 17. Serve.
Serving Suggestion: Serve the sandwich with a cauliflower bacon salad on the side.
Variation Tip: you can add a lettuce leaf to the filling as well.
Nutritional Information Per Serving: Calories 380 | Fat 19g |Sodium 318mg | Carbs 9g | Fiber 5g | Sugar 3g | Protein 26g

Mexican Beans & Fried Egg Sandwich

Prep time: 15 minutes | Cook Time: 15 minutes | Serves: 1

Ingredients:

Mexican-style simple syrup
¾ cup Piloncillo sugar
½ cup water
½ cup whole cloves

Sandwich
¼ cup refried beans
½ teaspoon chili powder
2 teaspoons olive oil
1 hamburger bun, split
1 fried egg

Peel of 1 orange
4 cinnamon sticks
1 raw almond, chopped

¼ sliced avocado
2 slices crispy bacon
Hot sauce, for garnish
Fresh cilantro, for garnish

Preparation:

1. Add sugar, water, whole cloves, orange peel, cinnamon sticks and almonds to a saucepan. 2. Cook for 10 minutes on low heat, then strain. 3. Preheat your Hamilton Beach Breakfast Sandwich Maker until PREHEAT light gets green. 4. Lift the top cover, ring, and cooking plate. 5. Place half of the English muffin, cut-side up, inside the bottom tray of the sandwich maker. 6. Spread the prepared syrup, refried beans and the rest of the ingredients on top. 7. Now lower the cooking plate and top rings. 8. Place the other top half of the muffin on top. 9. Cover the top hood, and let the sandwich cook for 5 minutes. 10. Rotate the handle of the cooking plate clockwise until it stops. 11. Lift the hood, the rings and transfer the sandwich to a plate. 12. Serve.
Serving Suggestion: Serve the sandwich with crispy bacon and your favorite sauce on the side.
Variation Tip: you can add a lettuce leaf to the filling as well.
Nutritional Information Per Serving: Calories 373 | Fat 8g |Sodium 146mg | Carbs 8g | Fiber 5g | Sugar 1g | Protein 23g

Mayo Avocado and Vegetables Sandwich

Prep time: 15 minutes | Cook Time: 5 minutes | Serves: 2

Ingredients:

¼ cup chives, chopped
¼ cup mayonnaise
¼ cup tarragon
¼ cup Greek yoghurt
1 lemon, halved
2 tablespoons olive oil
Sat and black pepper, to taste

½ head of butter lettuce, leaves torn
¼ English cucumber, sliced
1 avocado, sliced
4 slices grainy bread, cut into 4 inches' round
8 ounces mozzarella, sliced
2 cups alfalfa sprouts

Preparation:

1. Beat yoghurt with mayonnaise, tarragon, chives, black pepper and salt. 2. Preheat your Hamilton Beach Breakfast Sandwich Maker until PREHEAT light gets green. 3. Lift the top cover, ring, and cooking plate. 4. Place one bread slice inside the bottom tray of the sandwich maker. 5. Add ¼ lettuce, cucumber, avocado and the rest of the fillings. 6. Now lower the cooking plate and top rings. 7. Place another bread slice on top, then brush it with oil. 8. Cover the top hood, and let the sandwich cook for 5 minutes. 9. Rotate the handle of the cooking plate clockwise until it stops. 10. Lift the hood, the rings and transfer the sandwich to a plate. 11. Repeat the same steps with the remaining ingredients. 12. Serve.

Serving Suggestion: Serve the sandwich with crispy zucchini fries on the side.
Variation Tip: you can add a lettuce leaves to the filling as well.
Nutritional Information Per Serving: Calories 284 | Fat 7.9g |Sodium 704mg | Carbs 6g | Fiber 3.6g | Sugar 6g | Protein 18g

Beef Cheeseburger

Prep Time: 15 minutes | Cook Time: 7 minutes | Serves: 2

Ingredients:

Hamburger Pattie
2-pound minced beef
Salt and black pepper
3 onions, sliced into rings
Hamburger
4 soft hamburger buns, split in half
Lettuce, tomato slices

2 tablespoons oil
4 slices cheese

Ketchup, mustard, relish, sliced pickles

Preparation:

1. Separate beef into 4 equal portions. Form patties the size of your buns. 2. Season generously with salt and black pepper on both sides. Make a dent on one side. 3. Heat 1 tablespoon oil in a skillet over high heat. 4. Add onion and cook until wilted and caramelized. Season with salt and pepper, and then remove. 5. Heat 1 tablespoon oil in a suitable pan until smoking. 6. Add patties and cook for almost 2 minutes until deep golden with a great crust. 7. Preheat your Hamilton Beach Breakfast Sandwich Maker. 8. Lift the top cover, ring, and cooking plate. 9. Place the lower half of a bun in the sandwich maker. 10. Top it with ¼ ketchup, mustard, pickles and tomato slice. 11. Now lower the cooking plate and top rings then place a patty on top. 12. Place the other top half of the bun on top. 13. Cover the top hood, and let the sandwich cook for 5 minutes. 14. When finished cooking, rotate the handle of the cooking plate clockwise until it stops. 15. Lift the hood, the rings and transfer the sandwich to a plate. 16. Repeat the same with the remaining ingredients. 17. Serve.

Serving Suggestion: Serve the sandwich with coleslaw and your favorite sauce on the side.
Variation Tip: Add some additional dried herbs to the filling.
Nutritional Information Per Serving: Calories 229 | Fat 1.9 |Sodium 567mg | Carbs 1.9g | Fiber 0.4g | Sugar 0.6g | Protein 11.8g

Chapter 2 Red Meat Breakfast Sandwiches and Burgers

19   Mayo Beef Sandwiches

19   Beef and Giardiniera Sandwich

20   Crispy Chicken Sandwich

20   BBQ Pork Sandwich

21   Beef Mushroom Sandwich

21   Mayo Pork Sandwich

21   Bacon and Pineapple Cheese Sandwich

22   Beef Cabbage Burgers

22   Beef Patty Melts

23   Spicy Mayo Patty Melts

23   Smoky Steak and Cheeses Sandwich

24   Corned Beef and Coleslaw Sandwiches

24   Beef and Veggie Sandwich

24   Corned Beef and Sauerkraut Cheese Sandwich

25   Roasted Beef and Cheese Muffin Sandwich

25   Spiced Beef Onion Sandwiches

26   Flavorful Beef and Cheddar Sandwich

26   Simple Beef Patty Melt

27   Spiced Beef Hamburgers

27   Spicy Greens Cheddar Sandwich

Mayo Beef Sandwiches

Prep Time: 15 minutes | Cook Time: 30 minutes | Serves: 6

Ingredients:

1 red onion, sliced thinly
1 tablespoon, plus 2 teaspoons salt
6 tablespoons red wine vinegar
¾ cup mayonnaise
¾ cup sour cream
¼ cup plus 2 tablespoons jarred grated horseradish (with liquid)

½ teaspoon grated lemon zest
Freshly ground black pepper
Hot sauce
6 English muffins, cut in half
12 slices ripened tomatoes
24 ounces freshly sliced rare roast beef
3 cups watercress or arugula

Preparation:

1. In a small bowl, combine the onion and 1 tablespoon salt. Let sit for 20 minutes. 2. Rinse the onions under cold running water. Drain and squeeze to remove any excess liquid. 3. Mix the onions and the vinegar and marinate for not less than 30 minutes. 4. In a small bowl, mix together the mayonnaise, sour cream, black pepper, hot sauce, horseradish, zest, and 2 teaspoon salt. 5. Then refrigerate the horseradish sauce for about 30 minutes. 6. Preheat the Breakfast Sandwich Maker until the green PREHEAT light comes on. Lift cover, top ring, and cooking plate. 7. Place half of a muffin in the bottom ring of the sandwich maker. 8. Spread ⅙ of the filling ingredients on top except beef. 9. Lower cooking plate and top ring; place the ⅙th of the beef in the cooking plate. 10. Top with the other top half of a muffin. 11. Close the cover and cook for 5 minutes. Rotate the cooking plate handle clockwise until it stops. Then lift the cover and rings and carefully remove the sandwich with plastic spatula. 12. Repeat the process for the remaining ingredients. 13. Serve.

Serving Suggestion: Serve the sandwich with crispy bacon and your favorite sauce on the side.

Variation Tip: You can add a lettuce leave to the filling as well.

Nutritional Information Per Serving: Calories 260 | Fat 16g |Sodium 585mg | Carbs 3.1g | Fiber 1.3g | Sugar 0.2g | Protein 25.5g

Beef and Giardiniera Sandwich

Prep time: 15 minutes | Cook Time: 2 hours | Serves: 4

Ingredients:

1 ½ lbs. boneless beef chuck, cut into 2-inch pieces
Salt and black pepper to taste
1 tablespoon vegetable oil
6 garlic cloves, sliced
2 tablespoons white vinegar
1 tablespoon dried oregano
1 ½ teaspoons salt
1 teaspoon dried thyme

1 teaspoon dried rosemary
1 teaspoon black pepper
1 bay leaf
¼ teaspoon red pepper flakes
3 cups chicken broth
4 hamburger buns, sliced in half
1 cup chopped giardiniera (pickled Italian vegetables)
2 teaspoons chopped fresh flat-leaf parsley

Preparation:

1. In a deep skillet over medium heat, sear the beef with salt, black pepper and oil for 8 minutes until brown. 2. Stir in chicken broth, bay leaf, black pepper, red pepper flakes, thyme, rosemary, oregano, salt, vinegar and garlic. 3. Cover and simmer for 1½ hours. 4. Strain and shred cooked meat with a fork. 5. Place half of a bun, cut-side up, inside the bottom ring of the sandwich maker. 6. Lower cooking plate and top ring. Place ¼ beef and other ingredients in the cooking plate. 7. Top with the other half of the bun. 8. Close the cover and cook for 5 minutes. Rotate the cooking plate handle clockwise until it stops. Then lift the cover and rings and carefully remove the sandwich with plastic spatula. 9. Repeat the same with the remaining ingredients. 10. Serve.

Serving Suggestion: Serve the sandwich with a broccoli salad on the side.

Variation Tip: Enjoy sautéed veggies on the side for a change of taste.

Nutritional Information Per Serving: Calories 382 | Fat 4g |Sodium 232mg | Carbs 4g | Fiber 1g | Sugar 0g | Protein 21g

Crispy Chicken Sandwich

Prep time: 15 minutes | Cook Time: 35 minutes | Serves: 2

Ingredients:

Waffles

3 large eggs,
2 boxes cornbread mix
½ cup all-purpose flour
½ teaspoon baking soda

1 cup milk
2 tablespoons honey
4 tablespoons melted butter

Fried chicken

1-pound chicken cutlets, sliced in half
1 cup buttermilk
1 tablespoon hot sauce
1½ cup all-purpose flour
2 teaspoons garlic powder

1 teaspoon paprika
Kosher salt, to taste
Black pepper, to taste
Vegetable oil, for frying

Maple bourbon syrup

2 ounces bourbon whisky
8 ounces pure maple syrup

3 tablespoons butter

Preparation:

1. In a bowl, whisk together the maple syrup, butter and bourbon whisky. 2. In another bowl, toss the chicken with buttermilk and hot sauce. 3. Cover and marinate the chicken in the refrigerator for 30 minutes. 4. Combine all the waffle ingredients in a bowl and whisk until smooth. 5. Prepare a mini waffle maker by pouring in a small scoop of batter and cooking according to your waffle maker's instructions. 6. Make more small round waffles with the remaining batter and set aside. 7. In a bowl, mix together the flour, salt, garlic powder and paprika. 8. Coat the chicken with this flour mixture and shake off any excess. 9. Heat the oil in a deep frying pan over medium-high heat. 10. Fry the coated chicken until golden brown, then transfer to a plate with tongs. 11. Preheat the Breakfast Sandwich Maker until the green PREHEAT light comes on. Lift cover, top ring, and cooking plate. 12. Place one mini waffle in the bottom ring of the sandwich maker. 13. Lower cooking plate and top ring. Place a chicken cutlet inside the cooking plate. 14. Drizzle with a teaspoon of maple bourbon syrup mixture and place another mini waffle on top. 15. Close the cover and cook for 5 minutes. Rotate the cooking plate handle clockwise until it stops. Then lift the cover and rings and carefully remove the sandwich with plastic spatula. 16. Repeat the same steps with the remaining ingredients. 17. Serve.

Serving Suggestion: Serve the sandwich with a cauliflower bacon salad on the side.

Variation Tip: Add a layer of pickled onions for a change of taste.

Nutritional Information Per Serving: Calories 357 | Fat 12g |Sodium 48mg | Carbs 6g | Fiber 2g | Sugar 0g | Protein 24g

BBQ Pork Sandwich

Prep Time: 15 minutes | Cook Time: 4 hrs. 40 minutes | Serves: 4

Ingredients:

4 English muffins
14 ounces beef broth

3 pounds boneless pork ribs
18 ounces bottle barbeque sauce

Preparation:

1. Add pork and beef broth into the crock pot. 2. Cook on High for 4 hours. 3. When cooking time is up, break up the pork with a large fork. 4. Transfer the pork to a large pot then add in the BBQ sauce. Cook for about 35 minutes. 5. Use a fork to shred the cooked pork and set it aside. 6. Preheat the Breakfast Sandwich Maker until the green PREHEAT light comes on. Lift cover, top ring, and cooking plate. 7. Place half of a muffin in the bottom ring of the sandwich maker. 8. Lower cooking plate and top ring. Add ½ cup shredded pork to the cooking plate. 9. Top with another muffin half. 10. Close the cover and cook for 5 minutes. Rotate the cooking plate handle clockwise until it stops. Then lift the cover and rings and carefully remove the sandwich with plastic spatula. 11. Repeat the same steps with the remaining ingredients. 12. Serve.

Serving Suggestion: Serve the sandwich with coleslaw and your favorite sauce on the side.

Variation Tip: Add some additional ground black pepper to the filling.

Nutritional Information Per Serving: Calories 399 | Fat 16g |Sodium 537mg | Carbs 28g | Fiber 3g | Sugar 10g | Protein 35g

Beef Mushroom Sandwich

Prep Time: 15 minutes | Cook Time: 40 minutes | Serves: 4

Ingredients:

1 loaf hearty country bread, cut in 4-inch circle
3 tablespoon vegetable oil
3-pound boneless beef round steak, 2 inches thick
1 onion, sliced
2 cup sliced fresh mushrooms

1 garlic clove, minced
Salt to taste
Ground black pepper to taste
Garlic salt to taste

Preparation:

1. In a skillet over medium heat, fry your steak in 1 tablespoon of veggie oil for 6 minutes on each side and transfer to a plate. 2. Add 2 tablespoons of the vegetable oil and sauté the mushrooms, onion and garlic for 7 minutes, until the onion is transparent. 3. Preheat the Breakfast Sandwich Maker until the green PREHEAT light comes on. Lift cover, top ring, and cooking plate. 4. Place one bread slice in the bottom ring of the sandwich maker and add butter on top. 5. Lower cooking plate and top ring. Add ¼ of the rest of the fillings to the cooking plate. 6. Top with another bread slice. 7. Close the cover and cook for 5 minutes. Rotate the cooking plate handle clockwise until it stops. Then lift the cover and rings and carefully remove the sandwich with plastic spatula. 8. Repeat the same steps with the remaining ingredients. 9. Serve.

Serving Suggestion: Serve the sandwich with your favorite sauce on the side.
Variation Tip: Add some additional dried herbs to the filling.
Nutritional Information Per Serving: Calories 305 | Fat 15g |Sodium 482mg | Carbs 17g | Fiber 3g | Sugar 2g | Protein 35g

Mayo Pork Sandwich

Prep Time: 15 minutes | Cook Time: 5 minutes | Serves: 1

Ingredients:

Choice of greens
3 tablespoons mayonnaise
⅛ piece red bell pepper, sliced

2 sliced Gardenia loaf bread, cut in 4-inch circle
4 pounds pork strips

Preparation:

1. In a skillet over medium heat, cook the pork strips and bell peppers until tender. 2. Preheat the Breakfast Sandwich Maker until the green PREHEAT light comes on. Lift cover, top ring, and cooking plate. 3. Place one bread slice in the bottom ring of the sandwich maker and spread mayonnaise on top. 4. Lower cooking plate and top ring. Place ¼ cup pork, peppers and greens inside the cooking plate. 5. Top with another bread slice. 6. Close the cover and cook for 5 minutes. Rotate the cooking plate handle clockwise until it stops. Then lift the cover and rings and carefully remove the sandwich with plastic spatula. 7. Repeat the same steps with the remaining ingredients. 8. Serve.

Serving Suggestion: Serve the sandwich with crispy bacon and your favorite sauce on the side.
Variation Tip: You can add a drizzle of paprika on top of the filling as well.
Nutritional Information Per Serving: Calories 336 | Fat 6g |Sodium 181mg | Carbs 1.3g | Fiber 0.2g | Sugar 0.4g | Protein 69.2g

Bacon and Pineapple Cheese Sandwich

Prep Time: 15 minutes | Cook Time: 20 minutes | Serves: 4

Ingredients:

16 bacon slices
8 slices toasted white bread, cut in 4-inch circle

20 ounces sliced pineapple, drained
8 slices Cheddar cheese

Preparation:

1. Preheat the Breakfast Sandwich Maker until the green PREHEAT light comes on. Lift cover, top ring, and cooking plate. 2. Place one of the bread slice in the bottom ring of the sandwich maker. 3. Top it with a cheese slice and bacon. 4. Lower the cooking plate and top ring. Place ¼ of the pineapple slice on top. 5. Then top with another bread slice. 6. Close the cover and cook for 5 minutes. Rotate the cooking plate handle clockwise until it stops. Then lift the cover and rings and carefully remove the sandwich with plastic spatula. 7. Repeat the same with the remaining ingredients. 8. Serve.

Serving Suggestion: Serve the sandwich with your favorite sauce on the side.
Variation Tip: You can add a lettuce leave to the filling as well.
Nutritional Information Per Serving: Calories 348 | Fat 30g |Sodium 660mg | Carbs 5g | Fiber 0g | Sugar 0g | Protein 14g

Beef Cabbage Burgers

Prep time: 15 minutes | Cook Time: 1 hour | Serves: 8

Ingredients:

8 English muffins
1 lb. ground beef
4 teaspoons water
½ large head cabbage, chopped

½ large onion, chopped
1 garlic clove, chopped
Salt and black pepper to taste
1 tablespoon butter, melted

Preparation:

1. In a skillet over medium heat, sauté beef with onion, butter, black pepper, chopped clove and salt for 10 minutes. 2. Add the cabbage and water, then cook on low heat for 10 minutes. 3. Transfer the beef and cabbage mixture to a bowl and set aside. 4. Preheat the Breakfast Sandwich Maker until the green PREHEAT light comes on. Lift cover, top ring, and cooking plate. 5. Place half of the English muffin, cut-side up, inside the bottom ring of the sandwich maker. 6. Lower cooking plate and top ring. Add ⅛ of the beef mixture to the cooking plate. 7. Top with the other top half of the muffin. 8. Close the cover and cook for 5 minutes. Rotate the cooking plate handle clockwise until it stops. Then lift the cover and rings and carefully remove the sandwich with plastic spatula. 9. Repeat the same steps with the remaining muffins and ingredients. 10. Serve.

Serving Suggestion: Serve the sandwich with crispy sweet potato fries on the side.

Variation Tip: Add a layer of spicy mayo and pickled veggies for a change of taste.

Nutritional Information Per Serving: Calories 418 | Fat 22g |Sodium 350mg | Carbs 2.2g | Fiber 0.7g | Sugar 1g | Protein 24.3g

Beef Patty Melts

Prep time: 15 minutes | Cook Time: 20 minutes | Serves: 4

Ingredients:

1 lb. ground sirloin
1 tablespoon Worcestershire sauce
2 garlic cloves, minced, or more to taste
½ teaspoon salt
½ teaspoon black pepper
3 tablespoons unsalted butter

3 tablespoons olive oil
2 medium onions, sliced
4 slices cheddar cheese
4 teaspoons Dijon mustard
8 slices rye bread, cut into 4 inches round

Preparation:

1. In a food processor, Pulse beef with garlic, onion, black pepper, salt, butter and Worcestershire sauce for 1 minute. 2. Shape this mixture into 4 equal-sized patties. 3. In a skillet over medium heat, sear the patties with oil for 5 minutes per side. 4. Preheat the Breakfast Sandwich Maker until the green PREHEAT light comes on. Lift cover, top ring, and cooking plate. 5. Place one bread slice inside the bottom ring of the sandwich maker then spread 1 teaspoon mustard on top. 6. Top with a beef patty and a cheese slice. 7. Lower cooking plate and top ring. Place another bread slice in the cooking plate. 8. Close the cover and cook for 5 minutes. Rotate the cooking plate handle clockwise until it stops. Then lift the cover and rings and carefully remove the sandwich with plastic spatula. 9. Repeat the same with the remaining ingredients. 10. Serve.

Serving Suggestion: Serve the sandwich with a broccoli salad on the side.

Variation Tip: Add a layer of pickled onions for a change of taste.

Nutritional Information Per Serving: Calories 384 | Fat 25g |Sodium 460mg | Carbs 6g | Fiber 0.4g | Sugar 2g | Protein 26g

Spicy Mayo Patty Melts

Prep time: 15 minutes | Cook Time: 26 minutes | Serves: 3

Ingredients:

1 lb. ground beef
3 tablespoons chili seasoning mix
2 chipotle peppers in adobo sauce, minced
½ fluid ounce beer

¼ cup mayonnaise
1 chipotle pepper in adobo sauce, minced
6 (1 ounce) slices white bread, cut into 4 inches round
6 (½ ounce) slices pepper jack cheese

Preparation:

1. In a food processor, pulse the beef with chili seasoning mix, 2 chipotle peppers, and beer for about 1 minute. 2. Shape this mixture into 3 equal-sized patties. 3. In a skillet over medium heat, sear the patties for 5 minutes on each side. 4. Preheat the Breakfast Sandwich Maker until the green PREHEAT light comes on. Lift cover, top ring, and cooking plate. 5. Place one bread slice inside the bottom ring of the sandwich maker. Spread ¼ mayonnaise and chipotle pepper on top. 6. Lower the cooking plate and top ring. 7. Place a beef patty and 2 cheese slices in the cooking plate. Top with another bread slice. 8. Close the cover and cook for 5 minutes. Rotate the cooking plate handle clockwise until it stops. Then lift the cover and rings and carefully remove the sandwich with plastic spatula. 9. Repeat the same with the remaining ingredients. 10. Serve.

Serving Suggestion: Serve the sandwich with crispy fries on the side.

Variation Tip: you can add a lettuce leaf to the filling as well.

Nutritional Information Per Serving: Calories 419 | Fat 13g |Sodium 432mg | Carbs 9.1g | Fiber 3g | Sugar 1g | Protein 33g

Smoky Steak and Cheeses Sandwich

Prep time: 15 minutes | Cook Time: 15 minutes | Serves: 4

Ingredients:

4 hamburger buns, split
½ cup mayonnaise
3 garlic cloves, minced
1 tablespoon parmesan cheese
3 tablespoons olive oil
2 lbs. round steak, sliced

1 large onion, sliced and quartered
½ teaspoon Worcestershire sauce
1 pinch coarse sea salt
⅛ teaspoon liquid smoke
8 (1 ounce) slices of provolone cheese
½ teaspoon Italian seasoning

Preparation:

1. Sauté steak slices with onion, oil, garlic, salt, smoke, Italian seasoning, and Worcestershire sauce for 10 minutes. 2. Preheat your Hamilton Beach Breakfast Sandwich Maker until PREHEAT light gets green. 3. Lift the top cover, ring, and cooking plate. 4. Place half of a bun, cut-side up, inside the bottom tray of the sandwich maker. 5. Now lower the cooking plate and top rings, then add ¼ beef and the left ingredients on top. 6. Place the other top half of the bun on top. 7. Cover the top hood, and let the sandwich cook for 5 minutes. 8. Rotate the handle of the cooking plate clockwise until it stops. 9. Lift the hood, the rings and transfer the sandwich to a plate. 10. Repeat the same with the remaining ingredients. 11. Serve.

Serving Suggestion: Serve the sandwich with crispy fries on the side.

Variation Tip: you can add a lettuce leaf to the filling as well.

Nutritional Information Per Serving: Calories 335 | Fat 25g |Sodium 122mg | Carbs 3g | Fiber 0.4g | Sugar 1g | Protein 33g

Corned Beef and Coleslaw Sandwiches

Prep Time: 15 minutes | Cook Time: 5 minutes | Serves: 4

Ingredients:

8 slices rye bread, cut in 4-inch circle
1½ cup deli coleslaw
10 ounces deli corned beef (thinly sliced)

5 slices deli Swiss cheese
⅓ cup salad dressing

Preparation:

1. Preheat your Hamilton Beach Breakfast Sandwich Maker. 2. Lift the top cover, ring, and cooking plate. 3. Place one bread slice in the sandwich maker then top it with ¼ the coleslaw. 4. Now lower the cooking plate and top rings then place ¼ beef, cheese and dressing on top. 5. Add another bread slice on top. 6. Cover the top hood, and let the sandwich cook for 5 minutes. 7. When finished cooking, rotate the handle of the cooking plate clockwise until it stops. 8. Lift the hood, the rings and transfer the sandwich to a plate. 9. Repeat the same steps with the remaining ingredients. 10. Serve.
Serving Suggestion: Serve the sandwich with your favorite sauce on the side.
Variation Tip: You can add a lettuce leave to the filling as well.
Nutritional Information Per Serving: Calories 354; Fat 7.9g; Sodium 704mg; Carbs 6g; Fiber 3.6g; Sugar 6g; Protein 18g

Beef and Veggie Sandwich

Prep Time: 15 minutes | Cook Time: 5 minutes | Serves: 2

Ingredients:

1 cup chopped cooked beef
2 stalks celery, chopped
1 carrot, diced
¼ cup chopped onion
3 tablespoons mayonnaise

¼ teaspoons salt
⅛ teaspoons ground black pepper
⅛ teaspoons garlic powder
2 sesame seed buns, toasted until the broiler
2 eggs

Preparation:

1. **Get a bowl, combine:** garlic powder, beef, black pepper, celery, salt, carrot, mayo, and onion. Stir the mix until it is even. 2. Preheat your Hamilton Beach Breakfast Sandwich Maker. 3. Lift the top cover, ring, and cooking plate. 4. Place the lower half of the muffin in the sandwich maker and top with ½ of the remaining fillings. 5. Now lower the cooking plate and top rings, then pour in ½ of the egg. 6. Add another bun half on top. 7. Cover the top hood, and let the sandwich cook for 5 minutes. 8. When finished cooking, rotate the handle of the cooking plate clockwise until it stops. 9. Lift the hood, the rings and transfer the sandwich to a plate. 10. Repeat the same steps with the remaining ingredients. 11. Enjoy on toasted sesame seed buns.
Serving Suggestion: Serve the sandwich with coleslaw and your favorite sauce on the side.
Variation Tip: Add some additional ground black pepper to the filling.
Nutritional Information Per Serving: Calories 308 | Fat 24g |Sodium 715mg | Carbs 0.8g | Fiber 0.1g | Sugar 0.1g | Protein 21.9g

Corned Beef and Sauerkraut Cheese Sandwich

Prep Time: 15 minutes | Cook Time: 5 minutes | Serves: 4

Ingredients:

4 English muffins, sliced
1 tablespoon butter
4 slices cheese

½ cup drained sauerkraut
4 slices deli sliced corned beef
¼ cup dressing

Preparation:

1. Preheat your Hamilton Beach Breakfast Sandwich Maker. 2. Lift the top cover, ring, and cooking plate. 3. Place the lower half of the muffin in the sandwich maker. 4. Top the muffin with ¼ of the butter, cheese, sauerkraut. 5. Now lower the cooking plate and top rings then top it with ¼ beef and pour in the ¼ dressing. 6. Cover the top hood, and let the sandwich cook for 5 minutes. 7. When finished cooking, rotate the handle of the cooking plate clockwise until it stops. 8. Lift the hood, the rings and transfer the sandwich to a plate. 9. Repeat the same with the remaining ingredients. 10. Serve.
Serving Suggestion: Serve the sandwich with your favorite sauce on the side.
Variation Tip: Add some additional dried herbs to the filling.
Nutritional Information Per Serving: Calories 266 | Fat 6.3g |Sodium 193mg | Carbs 39.1g | Fiber 7.2g | Sugar 5.2g | Protein 14.8g

Roasted Beef and Cheese Muffin Sandwich

Prep Time: 15 minutes | Cook Time: 5 minutes | Serves: 4

Ingredients:

1 (10.5 ounces) can beef consommé
1 cup water
1 pound sliced deli roast beef

8 slices provolone cheese
4 English muffins, split

Preparation:

1. Open your buns and place them in a casserole dish. 2. Now combine water and beef consommé in a pan to make a broth. 3. Cook your beef in this mixture for 5 minutes. 4. Preheat your Hamilton Beach Breakfast Sandwich Maker. 5. Lift the top cover, ring, and cooking plate. 6. Place the lower half of the muffin in the sandwich maker. 7. Now lower the cooking plate and top rings, then add ¼ of the beef and cheese on top. 8. Add the other top half of the muffin on top. 9. Cover the top hood, and let the sandwich cook for 5 minutes. 10. When finished cooking, rotate the handle of the cooking plate clockwise until it stops. 11. Lift the hood, the rings and transfer the sandwich to a plate. 12. Repeat the same steps with the remaining ingredients. 13. Serve.

Serving Suggestion: Serve the sandwich with crispy bacon and your favorite sauce on the side.

Variation Tip: You can add a lettuce leave to the filling as well.

Nutritional Information Per Serving: Calories 380 | Fat 29g |Sodium 821mg | Carbs 34.6g | Fiber 0g | Sugar 0g | Protein 30g

Spiced Beef Onion Sandwiches

Prep Time: 15 minutes | Cook Time: 5 minutes | Serves: 3

Ingredients:

1 tablespoon vegetable oil
1½ pound boneless beef sirloin steak, sliced
1 onion, sliced
3 garlic cloves, minced
3 large celery ribs, sliced

3 tablespoons minced fresh ginger root
2 tablespoons soy sauce
1 teaspoon chili oil
6 English muffins, split

Preparation:

1. In a large skillet; heat vegetable oil on medium-high heat. 2. Then, stir in sirloin strips and sauté a few minutes until the strips starts to brown. 3. Next, stir in onion and garlic; sauté for about 2 minutes. 4. Add in the celery and ginger, keep on cooking for about 3 minutes or until the onion has softened. 5. Now, season it with soy sauce and chili oil. 6. Preheat your Hamilton Beach Breakfast Sandwich Maker. 7. Place the lower half of the muffin in the sandwich maker. 8. Now lower the cooking plate and top rings then add ⅓ of the fillings. 9. Add the other top half of the muffin on top. 10. Cover the top hood, and let the sandwich cook for 5 minutes. 11. When finished cooking, rotate the handle of the cooking plate clockwise until it stops. 12. Lift the hood, the rings and transfer the sandwich to a plate. 13. Repeat the same steps with the remaining ingredients. 14. Serve.

Serving Suggestion: Serve the sandwich with your favorite sauce on the side.

Variation Tip: Add some additional dried herbs to the filling.

Nutritional Information Per Serving: Calories 275 | Fat 1.4g |Sodium 582mg | Carbs 31.5g | Fiber 1.1g | Sugar 0.1g | Protein 29.8g

Flavorful Beef and Cheddar Sandwich

Prep Time: 15 minutes | Cook Time: 5 minutes | Serves: 4

Ingredients:

1-pound loaf French or Italian-style bread, cut in 4-inch circle
¼ cup minced green onions
1 tablespoon milk
⅛ teaspoon garlic powder
1 green bell pepper, sliced in rings
1-pound ground beef

1 cup sour cream
1 teaspoon Worcestershire sauce
¾ teaspoon salt
2 tablespoons butter, softened
2 tomatoes, sliced
1 cup shredded Cheddar cheese

Preparation:

1. Fry your beef and onions and remove any excess oils. 2. Now add in the following to the mix: pepper, milk, salt, garlic, Worcestershire sauce, garlic, and sour cream. 3. Preheat your Hamilton Beach Breakfast Sandwich Maker. 4. Lift the top cover, ring, and cooking plate. 5. Place one bread slice in the sandwich maker then add ¼ of the butter on top. 6. Now lower the cooking plate and top rings then add ¼ of the rest of the fillings. 7. Place another bread slice on top. 8. Cover the top hood, and let the sandwich cook for 5 minutes. 9. When finished cooking, rotate the handle of the cooking plate clockwise until it stops. 10. Lift the hood, the rings and transfer the sandwich to a plate. 11. Repeat the same steps with the remaining ingredients. 12. Serve.
Serving Suggestion: Serve the sandwich with crispy bacon and your favorite sauce on the side.
Variation Tip: You can add a layer of your favorite sauce to the filling as well.
Nutritional Information Per Serving: Calories 354; Fat 7.9g; Sodium 704mg; Carbs 6g; Fiber 3.6g; Sugar 6g; Protein 18g

Simple Beef Patty Melt

Prep time: 15 minutes | Cook Time: 15 minutes | Serves: 3

Ingredients:

1 lb. ground beef
½ teaspoon salt
¼ teaspoon ground black pepper
2 tablespoons butter

1 large onion, sliced
6 teaspoons mayonnaise
6 slices rye bread, cut into 4 inches round
6 slices sharp cheddar cheese

Preparation:

1. Mix beef with black pepper, salt, butter and onion in a food processor for 1 minute. 2. Make 6 equal-sized patties out of this mixture. 3. Sear the patties in a skillet for 5 minutes per side. 4. Preheat your Hamilton Beach Breakfast Sandwich Maker until PREHEAT light gets green. 5. Lift the top cover, ring, and cooking plate. 6. Place one bread slice inside the bottom tray of the sandwich maker then spread 1 teaspoon mayonnaise on top. 7. Place a beef patty and a cheese slice on top of the mayo. 8. Now lower the cooking plate and top rings. 9. Place another bread slice on top. 10. Cover the top hood, and let the sandwich cook for 5 minutes. 11. Rotate the handle of the cooking plate clockwise until it stops. 12. Lift the hood, the rings and transfer the sandwich to a plate. 13. Repeat the same with the remaining ingredients. 14. Serve.
Serving Suggestion: Serve the sandwich with crispy zucchini fries on the side.
Variation Tip: Add a layer of pickled veggies for a change of taste.
Nutritional Information Per Serving: Calories 445 | Fat 7.9g |Sodium 581mg | Carbs 4g | Fiber 2.6g | Sugar 0.1g | Protein 42.5g

Spiced Beef Hamburgers

Prep time: 15 minutes | Cook Time: 15 minutes | Serves: 2

Ingredients:

1 lb. beef sirloin, cut into thin 2 inch strips
½ teaspoon salt
½ teaspoon black pepper
½ teaspoon paprika
½ teaspoon chili powder
½ teaspoon onion powder
½ teaspoon garlic powder
½ teaspoon dried thyme

½ teaspoon dried marjoram
½ teaspoon dried basil
3 tablespoons vegetable oil
1 onion, sliced
1 green bell pepper, julienned
3 ounces Swiss cheese, sliced
4 hamburger buns, split lengthwise

Preparation:

1. Sauté beef with all the spices, herbs, oil, onion and bell pepper in a skillet for 10 minutes. 2. Preheat your Hamilton Beach Breakfast Sandwich Maker until PREHEAT light gets green. 3. Lift the top cover, ring, and cooking plate. 4. Place half of a bun, cut-side up, inside the bottom tray of the sandwich maker. 5. Now lower the cooking plate and top rings then add ¼ of the beef mixture. 6. Place the cheese and other top half of a bun on top. 7. Cover the top hood, and let the sandwich cook for 5 minutes. 8. Rotate the handle of the cooking plate clockwise until it stops. 9. Lift the hood, the rings and transfer the sandwich to a plate. 10. Repeat the same steps with the remaining ingredients. 11. Serve.

Serving Suggestion: Serve the sandwich with crispy carrot chips on the side.

Variation Tip: you can add a lettuce leaf to the filling as well.

Nutritional Information Per Serving: Calories 401 | Fat 7g |Sodium 269mg | Carbs 5g | Fiber 4g | Sugar 12g | Protein 26g

Spicy Greens Cheddar Sandwich

Prep time: 15 minutes | Cook Time: 12 minutes | Serves: 4

Ingredients:

1 bunch Lacinato kale
1 bunch mustard greens
10 tablespoons Irish butter
2 garlic cloves, minced
¾ cup sliced green onions, white and light green parts only

Salt and black pepper to taste
1 pinch cayenne pepper, or to taste
2 tablespoons seasoned rice vinegar
8 thick slices of French bread, cut into 4 inches round
1 (8 ounces) package Irish white cheddar cheese, sliced

Preparation:

1. Sauté kale with greens, butter, garlic, green onions, black pepper, salt and cayenne pepper and rice vinegar in a skillet for 7 minutes. 2. Preheat your Hamilton Beach Breakfast Sandwich Maker until PREHEAT light gets green. 3. Lift the top cover, ring, and cooking plate. 4. Place one bread slice inside the bottom tray of the sandwich maker. 5. Now lower the cooking plate and top rings, then add ¼ of the kale mixture. 6. Place a cheese slice and the other bread slice on top. 7. Cover the top hood, and let the sandwich cook for 5 minutes. 8. Rotate the handle of the cooking plate clockwise until it stops. 9. Lift the hood, the rings and transfer the sandwich to a plate. 10. Repeat the same step with the remaining ingredients. 11. Serve.

Serving Suggestion: Serve the sandwich with a cauliflower bacon salad on the side.

Variation Tip: Add a layer of sliced bell peppers for a change of taste.

Nutritional Information Per Serving: Calories 361 | Fat 16g |Sodium 189mg | Carbs 3g | Fiber 0.3g | Sugar 18.2g | Protein 33.3g

Chapter 3 Eggs Breakfast Sandwich Recipes

29   Cheese Egg Buttermilk Biscuit Sandwich

29   BLT Egg Sandwich

29   Japanese Egg Sandwich

30   Ham and Olive Sandwich

30   Marinara Parmesan Egg Muffin

30   Asparagus-Prosciutto Muffin Sandwich

31   Spinach and Ham Sandwich

31   Cheese Egg & Beans Muffin Sandwich

31   Celery and Egg Salad Sandwich

32   Sausage Breading Pudding Sandwich

32   Chorizo Avocado Sandwich

32   Cheese Spinach and Egg Sandwich

33   Egg and Red Pepper Cheese Sandwich

33   Fried Egg Cheese Sandwich

33   Green Peas and Egg Sandwiches

34   Butter Egg and Cheese Bagel

34   Egg Whites and Mozzarella Cheese Muffin

34   Mayo Egg Sandwich

35   Egg Salad Muffin Sandwich

35   Egg-and-Ham Sandwich with Hummus

36   Cheese Zucchini Sandwich

36   Egg, Anchovy and Ham Hamburgers

37   Fried Egg, Tomato and Avocado Sandwich

Cheese Egg Buttermilk Biscuit Sandwich

Prep Time: 15 minutes | Cook Time: 5 minutes | Serves: 1

Ingredients:

1 buttermilk biscuit, cut in half
1 slice of sharp cheddar cheese
1 egg

Milk
Salt and black pepper to taste

Preparation:

1. Crack the egg to a bowl and add a bit of milk. Season with a dash of salt and black pepper. Whisk well. 2. Preheat the Breakfast Sandwich Maker until the green PREHEAT light comes on. Lift cover, top ring, and cooking plate. 3. Place half of the biscuit in the bottom ring of the sandwich maker, then add cheese. 4. Lower the cooking plate and top ring, then pour the egg mixture into the cooking plate. 5. Top with the other half of the biscuit. 6. Close the cover and cook for 5 minutes. Rotate the cooking plate handle clockwise until it stops. Then lift the cover and rings and carefully remove the sandwich with plastic spatula. 7. Serve.

Serving Suggestion: Serve the sandwich with crispy bacon and your favorite sauce on the side.

Variation Tip: Add some additional dried herbs to the filling.

Nutritional Information Per Serving: Calories 268 | Fat 10.4g |Sodium 411mg | Carbs 0.4g | Fiber 0.1g | Sugar 0.1g | Protein 40.6g

BLT Egg Sandwich

Prep Time: 15 minutes | Cook Time: 5 minutes | Serves: 1

Ingredients:

3 bacon slices, cooked
1 egg
1 pita bread, cut in half, cut in 4-inch circle

1 slice tomato
2 leaves romaine lettuce
2 tablespoons yogurt

Preparation:

1. Preheat the Breakfast Sandwich Maker until the green PREHEAT light comes on. Lift cover, top ring, and cooking plate. 2. Place one half of the pita bread in the bottom ring of the sandwich maker, then add yogurt, lettuce, bacon slices and tomato on top. 3. Lower the cooking plate and top ring. Add egg to cooking plate. Pierce yolk with a fork or toothpick. 4. Top with the other half of the bread. 5. Close the cover and cook for 5 minutes. Rotate the cooking plate handle clockwise until it stops. Then lift the cover and rings and carefully remove the sandwich with plastic spatula. 6. Serve.

Serving Suggestion: Serve the sandwich with your favorite sauce on the side.

Variation Tip: Add some additional ground black pepper to the filling.

Nutritional Information Per Serving: Calories 353 | Fat 5g |Sodium 818mg | Carbs 53.2g | Fiber 4.4g | Sugar 8g | Protein 17.3g

Japanese Egg Sandwich

Prep time: 15 minutes | Cook Time: 5 minutes | Serves: 1

Ingredients:

2 sandwich bread slices, cut into 4 inches round
3 medium-boiled eggs peeled, mash
1½ tablespoon Japanese mayonnaise
¼ teaspoon Dijon mustard

⅛ teaspoon white pepper
⅛ teaspoon onion powder
1 pinch salt

Preparation:

1. In a bowl, mix mayonnaise, white pepper, mustard, onion powder and salt. 2. Add in mashed eggs and stir to mix well. 3. Preheat your Hamilton Beach Breakfast Sandwich Maker until PREHEAT light gets green. 4. Lift the top cover, ring, and cooking plate. 5. Place a bread slice inside the bottom ring of the sandwich maker. 6. Top the bread with the egg mixture. 7. Lower the cooking plate and top ring. 8. Place a bread slice in the cooking plate. 9. Close the cover and cook for 5 minutes. Rotate the cooking plate handle clockwise until it stops. Then lift the cover and rings and carefully remove the sandwich with plastic spatula. 10. Serve.

Serving Suggestion: Serve the sandwich with crispy zucchini fries on the side.

Variation Tip: you can add a lettuce leaf to the filling as well.

Nutritional Information Per Serving: Calories 352 | Fat 2.4g |Sodium 216mg | Carbs 6g | Fiber 2.3g | Sugar 1.2g | Protein 27g

Ham and Olive Sandwich

Prep Time: 15 minutes | Cook Time: 5 minutes | Serves: 1

Ingredients:

1 slice ham, cooked
1 egg
2 slices French bread, cut in 4-inch circle

1 slice provolone cheese
1 tablespoon pimento-stuffed green olives, chopped
1 tablespoon roasted red bell pepper, drained and chopped

Preparation:

1. Preheat the Breakfast Sandwich Maker until the green PREHEAT light comes on. Lift cover, top ring, and cooking plate. 2. Place one of the bread slices in the bottom ring of the sandwich maker. Place the ham, cheese, green olives and red bell peppers on it. 3. Lower the cooking plate and top ring. Add egg to cooking plate. Pierce yolk with a fork or toothpick. 4. Top with the other circle of the bread. 5. Close the cover and cook for 5 minutes. Rotate the cooking plate handle clockwise until it stops. Then lift the cover and rings and carefully remove the sandwich with plastic spatula. 6. Serve.

Serving Suggestion: Serve the sandwich with coleslaw and your favorite sauce on the side.

Variation Tip: Add some additional dried herbs to the filling.

Nutritional Information Per Serving: Calories 456 | Fat 16.4g |Sodium 1321mg | Carbs 19.2g | Fiber 2.2g | Sugar 4.2g | Protein 55.2g

Marinara Parmesan Egg Muffin

Prep Time: 15 minutes | Cook Time: 5 minutes | Serves: 1

Ingredients:

1 English muffin (whole grain is best), split
1 large egg, beaten

⅛ cup of parmesan cheese
¼ cup of marinara sauce

Preparation:

1. Preheat the Breakfast Sandwich Maker until the green PREHEAT light comes on. Lift cover, top ring, and cooking plate. 2. Place half of the muffin in the sandwich maker and top with the sauce. 3. Sprinkle the parmesan cheese on top. 4. Lower the cooking plate and top ring, then pour in the beaten egg. 5. Top with another muffin half. 6. Close the cover and cook for 5 minutes. Rotate the cooking plate handle clockwise until it stops. Then lift the cover and rings and carefully remove the sandwich with plastic spatula. 7. Serve.

Serving Suggestion: Serve the sandwich with your favorite sauce on the side.

Variation Tip: You can add a layer of your favorite sauce to the filling as well.

Nutritional Information Per Serving: Calories 351 | Fat 11g |Sodium 150mg | Carbs 3.3g | Fiber 0.2g | Sugar 1g | Protein 33.2g

Asparagus-Prosciutto Muffin Sandwich

Prep Time: 15 minutes | Cook Time: 5 minutes | Serves: 1

Ingredients:

1 English muffin
3 slices prosciutto, sliced
3 asparagus stalks, broiled
1 teaspoon olive oil
2 tablespoons Greek yogurt, unflavored

1 teaspoon Dijon mustard
⅛ teaspoons lemon juice
Sea salt
Chives, snipped
1 egg

Preparation:

1. Combine yogurt, mustard and lemon juice in small cup and set aside. 2. Preheat the Breakfast Sandwich Maker until the green PREHEAT light comes on. Lift cover, top ring, and cooking plate. 3. Place half of the muffin in the bottom ring of the sandwich maker, then add asparagus and prosciutto on top. Drizzle with oil and sprinkle with salt. 4. Lower the cooking plate and top ring, then pour in the egg and top with chives. 5. Drizzle with the yogurt mixture. 6. Add the other half of the muffin on top. 7. Close the cover and cook for 5 minutes. Rotate the cooking plate handle clockwise until it stops. Then lift the cover and rings and carefully remove the sandwich with plastic spatula. 8. Serve.

Serving Suggestion: Serve the sandwich with your favorite sauce on the side.

Variation Tip: You can add a drizzle of lemon juice on top of the filling as well.

Nutritional Information Per Serving: Calories 346 | Fat 16.1g |Sodium 882mg | Carbs 1.3g | Fiber 0.5g | Sugar 0.5g | Protein 48.2g

Spinach and Ham Sandwich

Prep Time: 15 minutes | Cook Time: 5 minutes | Serves: 1

Ingredients:

1 English muffin
½ cup baby spinach, washed and chopped
1 teaspoon olive oil
1 slice Cheddar cheese

1 slice ham
1 egg
Fresh basil (optional)

Preparation:

1. Heat olive oil in a small sauté pan. Add spinach and sauté until just tender. Remove from heat. 2. In small bowl, stir the spinach and egg together with a fork. 3. Preheat the Breakfast Sandwich Maker until the green PREHEAT light comes on. Lift cover, top ring, and cooking plate. 4. Place half of the muffin in the bottom ring of the sandwich maker and top with cheese and ham. 5. Lower the cooking plate and top ring. Pour the spinach-egg mixture into the cooking plate. 6. Top with the other half of the muffin. 7. Close the cover and cook for 5 minutes. Rotate the cooking plate handle clockwise until it stops. Then lift the cover and rings and carefully remove the sandwich with plastic spatula. 8. Serve.

Serving Suggestion: Serve the sandwich with crispy bacon and your favorite sauce on the side.

Variation Tip: You can add a lettuce leave to the filling as well.

Nutritional Information Per Serving: Calories 502 | Fat 25g |Sodium 230mg | Carbs 1.5g | Fiber 0.2g | Sugar 0.4g | Protein 64.1g

Cheese Egg & Beans Muffin Sandwich

Prep Time: 15 minutes | Cook Time: 10 minutes | Serves: 2

Ingredients:

2 English muffins
1 ounce shredded Mexican cheese
2 tablespoons refried beans

2 large eggs
1 tablespoon sliced green onion

Preparation:

1. Preheat the Breakfast Sandwich Maker until the green PREHEAT light comes on. Lift cover, top ring, and cooking plate. 2. Place half of the muffin in the bottom ring of the sandwich maker. Then top with ½ of the refried beans and cheese. 3. lower the cooking plate and top ring. Add egg to cooking plate. Pierce yolk with a fork or toothpick. 4. Add green onion and top with the other half of the muffin. 5. Close the cover and cook for 5 minutes. Rotate the cooking plate handle clockwise until it stops. Then lift the cover and rings and carefully remove the sandwich with plastic spatula. 6. Repeat the same steps with the remaining ingredients. 7. Serve.

Serving Suggestion: Serve the sandwich with coleslaw and your favorite sauce on the side.

Variation Tip: You can add a drizzle of paprika on top of the filling as well.

Nutritional Information Per Serving: Calories 351 | Fat 16g |Sodium 777mg | Carbs 26g | Fiber 4g | Sugar 5g | Protein 28g

Celery and Egg Salad Sandwich

Prep time: 15 minutes | Cook Time: 5 minutes | Serves: 1

Ingredients:

1 hard-boiled large egg, peeled and chopped
2 tablespoons mayonnaise, to taste
2 tablespoons chopped celery
1 tablespoon chopped green onion or chives

1 pinch curry powder
Salt and black pepper to taste
1 Lettuce leaf
2 white bread slices, cut into 4 inches round

Preparation:

1. In a bowl, mix together the celery, green onion, mayonnaise, curry powder, black pepper and salt. 2. Preheat the Breakfast Sandwich Maker until the green PREHEAT light comes on. Lift cover, top ring, and cooking plate. 3. Place a bread slice inside the bottom ring of the sandwich maker. 4. Spread the mayonnaise mixture, lettuce leaf and chopped eggs on top. 5. Lower the cooking plate and top ring. 6. Place the other bread slice on top. 7. Close the cover and cook for 5 minutes. Rotate the cooking plate handle clockwise until it stops. Then lift the cover and rings and carefully remove the sandwich with plastic spatula. 8. Serve.

Serving Suggestion: Serve the sandwich with crispy bacon and your favorite sauce on the side.

Variation Tip: Add a layer of spicy mayo and pickled veggies for a change of taste.

Nutritional Information Per Serving: Calories 388 | Fat 8g |Sodium 611mg | Carbs 8g | Fiber 0 | Sugar 4g | Protein 13g

Sausage Breading Pudding Sandwich

Prep Time: 15 minutes | Cook Time: 7 minutes | Serves: 1

Ingredients:

2 slices stale bread, cubed
1 large egg
2 tablespoons maple syrup or honey
2 tablespoons plain yogurt
1 tablespoon melted butter

Pinch ground nutmeg
1 chicken sausage patty, cooked
1 slice Swiss cheese
1 large egg, beaten

Preparation:

1. Place the chunks of bread in a small round ramekin. 2. In a small bowl, whisk together an egg, maple syrup, yogurt, butter and nutmeg and pour over the bread carefully. 3. Microwave the ramekin on high for 2 minutes until the pudding is firm and hot. Allow it to cool for 5 minutes. 4. Preheat the Breakfast Sandwich Maker until the green PREHEAT light comes on. Lift cover, top ring, and cooking plate. 5. Remove the bread pudding from the ramekin and place half of bread pudding in the bottom ring of the breakfast sandwich maker. 6. Add the sausage patty and slice of Swiss cheese on top. 7. Lower cooking plate and top ring. Add the beaten egg to cooking plate. 8. Top with the other half of the bread pudding. 9. Close the cover and cook for 5 minutes. Rotate the cooking plate handle clockwise until it stops. Then lift the cover and rings and carefully remove the sandwich with plastic spatula. 10. Serve.

Serving Suggestion: Serve the sandwich with crispy bacon and your favorite sauce on the side.

Variation Tip: You can add a lettuce leave to the filling as well.

Nutritional Information Per Serving: Calories 379 | Fat 19g |Sodium 184mg | Carbs 12.3g | Fiber 0.6g | Sugar 2g | Protein 37.7g

Chorizo Avocado Sandwich

Prep Time: 15 minutes | Cook Time: 20 minutes | Serves: 4

Ingredients:

1 round flatbread, sliced, cut in 4-inch circle
1 chorizo sausage patty, cooked
½ avocado, cleaned, pitted and sliced

2 ounces Monterey jack, shredded
1 tablespoon feta cheese or queso fresco, crumbled
4 large eggs

Preparation:

1. Preheat the Breakfast Sandwich Maker until the green PREHEAT light comes on. Lift cover, top ring, and cooking plate. 2. Place one bread slice in the bottom ring of the sandwich maker then add cheese on top. 3. Lower the cooking plate and top ring. Crack an egg and add ¼th of the rest of the fillings to the cooking plate. 4. Top with another bread slice. 5. Close the cover and cook for 5 minutes. Rotate the cooking plate handle clockwise until it stops. Then lift the cover and rings and carefully remove the sandwich with plastic spatula. 6. Repeat the same steps with the remaining ingredients. 7. Serve.

Serving Suggestion: Serve the sandwich with your favorite sauce on the side.

Variation Tip: You can add a lettuce leave to the filling as well.

Nutritional Information Per Serving: Calories 374 | Fat 13g |Sodium 552mg | Carbs 25g | Fiber 1.2g | Sugar 1.2g | Protein 37.7g

Cheese Spinach and Egg Sandwich

Prep time: 15 minutes | Cook Time: 5 minutes | Serves: 1

Ingredients:

2 tablespoons pimiento cheese
1 whole-wheat English muffin, split and toasted
¼ cup baby spinach

1 large egg, scrambled
1 teaspoon hot sauce, such as tabasco

Preparation:

1. Preheat the Breakfast Sandwich Maker until the green PREHEAT light comes on. Lift cover, top ring, and cooking plate. 2. Place half of the English muffin, cut-side up, inside the bottom ring of the sandwich maker. 3. Add spinach, egg, hot sauce and cheese on top. 4. Lower the cooking plate and top ring. 5. Place the other top half of the muffin in the cooking plate. 6. Close the cover and cook for 5 minutes. Rotate the cooking plate handle clockwise until it stops. Then lift the cover and rings and carefully remove the sandwich with plastic spatula. 7. Serve.

Serving Suggestion: Serve the sandwich with crispy sweet potato fries on the side.

Variation Tip: you can add a lettuce leaf to the filling as well.

Nutritional Information Per Serving: Calories 380 | Fat 8g |Sodium 339mg | Carbs 5.6g | Fiber 1g | Sugar 2g | Protein 21g

Egg and Red Pepper Cheese Sandwich

Prep Time: 15 minutes | Cook Time: 5 minutes | Serves: 1

Ingredients:

2 slices multigrain bread, cut in 4-inch circle
1-ounce goat cheese
2 slices fresh red pepper

1 slice red onion
Salt and black pepper to taste
1 large egg, beaten

Preparation:

1. Preheat the Breakfast Sandwich Maker until the green PREHEAT light comes on. Lift cover, top ring, and cooking plate. 2. Place one bread slice in the bottom ring of the sandwich maker. 3. Add the goat cheese, red pepper and red onion on top. 4. Season with salt and black pepper. 5. Lower the cooking plate and top ring, then pour in the egg. 6. Top with the other circle of the bread. 7. Close the cover and cook for 5 minutes. Rotate the cooking plate handle clockwise until it stops. Then lift the cover and rings and carefully remove the sandwich with plastic spatula. 8. Serve.

Serving Suggestion: Serve the sandwich with your favorite sauce on the side.
Variation Tip: Add some additional ground black pepper to the filling.
Nutritional Information Per Serving: Calories 546 | Fat 33.1g |Sodium 1201mg | Carbs 30g | Fiber 2.4g | Sugar 9.7g | Protein 32g

Fried Egg Cheese Sandwich

Prep time: 15 minutes | Cook Time: 20 minutes | Serves: 4

Ingredients:

2 teaspoons butter
4 eggs
4 slices processed American cheese
8 slices white bread, cut into 4 inches round

Salt and pepper to taste
2 tablespoons mayonnaise
2 tablespoons ketchup

Preparation:

1. Melt the butter in a pan, crack in one egg and fry until set. 2. Transfer the egg to a plate and fry more eggs in the same way. 3. In a bowl mix ketchup, mayonnaise, black pepper and salt. 4. Preheat the Breakfast Sandwich Maker until the green PREHEAT light comes on. Lift cover, top ring, and cooking plate. 5. Place a bread slice inside the bottom ring of the sandwich maker and spread ¼th mayonnaise on top. 6. Lower the cooking plate and top ring. Place a fried egg in the cooking plate. 7. Top with the other bread slice. 8. Close the cover and cook for 5 minutes. Rotate the cooking plate handle clockwise until it stops. Then lift the cover and rings and carefully remove the sandwich with plastic spatula. 9. Make more sandwiches in the same way. 10. Serve.

Serving Suggestion: Serve the sandwich with a cauliflower bacon salad on the side.
Variation Tip: Enjoy sautéed veggies on the side for a change of taste.
Nutritional Information Per Serving: Calories 429 | Fat 17g |Sodium 422mg | Carbs 5g | Fiber 0g | Sugar 1g | Protein 41g

Green Peas and Egg Sandwiches

Prep time: 15 minutes | Cook Time: 10 minutes | Serves: 2

Ingredients:

2 cups chopped mustard greens
¼ cup toasted walnut oil
2 tablespoons apple cider vinegar
¼ teaspoon salt
¾ teaspoon black pepper

6 ounces frozen green peas, thawed
1 ½ ounces Parmigiano-Reggiano cheese, grated
1 tablespoon olive oil
4 large eggs, beaten
4 slices multigrain bread, cut into 4 inches' round

Preparation:

1. In a food processor, blend greens, walnut oil, black pepper, apple cider vinegar, salt and peas until smooth. 2. Preheat the Breakfast Sandwich Maker until the green PREHEAT light comes on. Lift cover, top ring, and cooking plate. 3. Place a bread slice inside the bottom ring of the sandwich maker. 4. Spread half of the olive oil and green pea pesto on top. 5. Lower the cooking plate and top ring. Pour in ½ of the egg into the cooking plate and add the cheese. 6. Top with another bread slice. 7. Close the cover and cook for 5 minutes. Rotate the cooking plate handle clockwise until it stops. Then lift the cover and rings and carefully remove the sandwich with plastic spatula. 8. Repeat the same steps with the remaining ingredients. 9. Serve.

Serving Suggestion: Serve the sandwich with a broccoli salad on the side.
Variation Tip: Add a layer of pickled onions for a change of taste.
Nutritional Information Per Serving: Calories 301 | Fat 16g |Sodium 412mg | Carbs 3g | Fiber 0.2g | Sugar 1g | Protein 28.2g

Butter Egg and Cheese Bagel

Prep Time: 15 minutes | Cook Time: 5 minutes | Serves: 1

Ingredients:

1 plain bagel, sliced

1 egg

1 pat of butter

1 slice of American cheese

Preparation:

1. Preheat your Hamilton Beach Breakfast Sandwich Maker. 2. Lift the top cover, ring, and cooking plate. 3. Place the lower half of the bagel in the sandwich maker and top with butter. 4. Place the slice of American cheese on top of the bagel bottom. 5. Now lower the cooking plate and top rings, then pour in the egg. 6. Cover the top hood, and let the sandwich cook for 5 minutes. 7. When finished cooking, rotate the handle of the cooking plate clockwise until it stops. 8. Lift the hood, the rings and transfer the sandwich to a plate. 9. Serve.

Serving Suggestion: Serve the sandwich with crispy bacon and your favorite sauce on the side.

Variation Tip: Add some additional ground black pepper to the filling.

Nutritional Information Per Serving: Calories 316 | Fat 12.2g |Sodium 587mg | Carbs 12.2g | Fiber 1g | Sugar 1.8g | Protein 25.8g

Egg Whites and Mozzarella Cheese Muffin

Prep Time: 15 minutes | Cook Time: 5 minutes | Serves: 1

Ingredients:

1 whole wheat English muffin, cut in half

2 large eggs, egg whites only

1 slice of low fat mozzarella cheese

Preparation:

1. Preheat your Hamilton Beach Breakfast Sandwich Maker. 2. Lift the top cover, ring, and cooking plate. 3. Place the lower half of the muffin in the sandwich maker. 4. Place the slice of low fat mozzarella cheese on the English muffin. 5. Next, in the egg cooking plate, add the egg whites. 6. Now lower the cooking plate and top rings then pour in the egg. 7. Place another muffin half on top. 8. Cover the top hood, and let the sandwich cook for 5 minutes. 9. When finished cooking, rotate the handle of the cooking plate clockwise until it stops. 10. Lift the hood, the rings and transfer the sandwich to a plate. 11. Serve.

Serving Suggestion: Serve the sandwich with your favorite sauce on the side.

Variation Tip: You can add a drizzle of lemon juice on top of the filling as well.

Nutritional Information Per Serving: Calories 336 | Fat 27.1g |Sodium 66mg | Carbs 1.1g | Fiber 0.4g | Sugar 0.2g | Protein 19.7g

Mayo Egg Sandwich

Prep time: 15 minutes | Cook Time: 5 minutes | Serves: 1

Ingredients:

2 slices bread, cut into 4 inches' round

1½ teaspoon olive oil

2 extra-large eggs

1 pinch kosher salt

2 teaspoons mayonnaise

1 teaspoon crushed Calabrian chilies

Preparation:

1. Beat eggs with salt and oil in a bowl. 2. Preheat your Hamilton Beach Breakfast Sandwich Maker until PREHEAT light gets green. 3. Lift the top cover, ring, and cooking plate. 4. Place a bread slice inside the bottom tray of the sandwich maker. 5. Spread mayonnaise on top of the bread. 6. Now lower the cooking plate and top rings then pour in the egg. 7. Add chilies and the other bread slice on top. 8. Cover the top hood, and let the sandwich cook for 5 minutes. 9. Rotate the handle of the cooking plate clockwise until it stops. 10. Lift the hood, the rings and transfer the sandwich to a plate. 11. Serve.

Serving Suggestion: Serve the sandwich with a broccoli salad on the side.

Variation Tip: you can add a lettuce leaf to the filling as well.

Nutritional Information Per Serving: Calories 376 | Fat 21g |Sodium 476mg | Carbs 2g | Fiber 3g | Sugar 4g | Protein 20g

Egg Salad Muffin Sandwich

Prep Time: 15 minutes | Cook Time: 5 minutes | Serves: 1

Ingredients:

2 whole grain English muffins, split
¼ cup of Greek yogurt
1 teaspoon of horseradish
2 teaspoons of honey
2 teaspoons of Dijon mustard

Black pepper to taste
Salt to taste
3 hard-boiled eggs, chopped roughly
⅓ cup of pepper jack cheese, shredded

Preparation:

1. In a bowl, combine together the Greek yogurt, horseradish, honey, Dijon mustard, pepper, salt and hard boiled eggs. Stir together until well combined. 2. Preheat your Hamilton Beach Breakfast Sandwich Maker. 3. Lift the top cover, ring, and cooking plate. 4. Place one bread slice in the sandwich maker. 5. Place about cheese on top of the English muffin bottom. 6. Then, spoon the egg salad mixture on top of the cheese. 7. Now lower the cooking plate and top rings. 8. Place another muffin half on top. 9. Cover the top hood, and let the sandwich cook for 5 minutes. 10. When finished cooking, rotate the handle of the cooking plate clockwise until it stops. 11. Lift the hood, the rings and transfer the sandwich to a plate. 12. Repeat with the rest of the ingredients. 13. Serve.

Serving Suggestion: Serve the sandwich with coleslaw and your favorite sauce on the side.
Variation Tip: Add some additional dried herbs to the filling.
Nutritional Information Per Serving: Calories 400 | Fat 32g |Sodium 721mg | Carbs 2.6g | Fiber 0g | Sugar 0g | Protein 27.4g

Egg-and-Ham Sandwich with Hummus

Prep time: 15 minutes | Cook Time: 5 minutes | Serves: 4

Ingredients:

Sandwich
4 tomatoes, seeded and diced
2 garlic cloves, chopped
Salt and black pepper, to taste
6 leaves basil, shredded
2 cups ham, smoked and diced
Hummus
2 cups chickpeas, cooked
½ cup tahini
¼ cup olive oil
1 garlic clove, crushed

8 eggs, beaten
Oil, of choice, for brushing
8 bread slices, cut into 4 inches' round
1 cup hummus
¼ cup olive oil

1 lemon, juiced
½ teaspoon salt
1 tablespoon cumin

Preparation:

1. Blend chickpeas with tahini, oil, garlic, lemon juice, salt and cumin in a food processor. 2. Preheat your Hamilton Beach Breakfast Sandwich Maker until PREHEAT light gets green. 3. Lift the top cover, ring, and cooking plate. 4. Place a bread slice inside the bottom tray of the sandwich maker. 5. Top the bread with ¼ hummus and spread it evenly. 6. Beat the eggs with a tomato slice, sham, garlic, black pepper, salt, olive oil and basil in a suitable bowl. 7. Now lower the cooking plate and top rings, then pour in ¼ of the egg. 8. Place another bread slice on top. 9. Cover the top hood, and let the sandwich cook for 5 minutes. 10. Rotate the handle of the cooking plate clockwise until it stops. 11. Lift the hood, the rings and transfer the sandwich to a plate. 12. Repeat the same steps with the remaining ingredients. Serve.

Serving Suggestion: Serve the sandwich with a cauliflower bacon salad on the side.
Variation Tip: Add a layer of spicy mayo and pickled veggies for a change of taste.
Nutritional Information Per Serving: Calories 431 | Fat 20.1g |Sodium 364mg | Carbs 3g | Fiber 1g | Sugar 1.4g | Protein 15g

Cheese Zucchini Sandwich

Prep time: 15 minutes | Cook Time: 10 minutes | Serves: 4

Ingredients:

½ large red onion, sliced
3 bell peppers, sliced
1 medium zucchini, sliced
2 tablespoons olive oil
1 teaspoon minced garlic
1 teaspoon coarse sea salt

¼ teaspoon black pepper
½ teaspoon cumin powder
8 slices white bread, cut into 4 inches' round
¼ cup chimichurri sauce
8 slices mozzarella cheese

Preparation:

1. Sauté red onion, bell peppers, zucchini, olive oil, garlic, sea salt, black pepper, and cumin powder in a skillet for 5 minutes. 2. Preheat your Hamilton Beach Breakfast Sandwich Maker until PREHEAT light gets green. 3. Lift the top cover, ring, and cooking plate. 4. Place a bread slice inside the bottom tray of the sandwich maker. 5. Spread chimichurri sauce, zucchini mixture and a mozzarella cheese slice on top. 6. Now lower the cooking plate and top rings. 7. Place another bread slice on top. 8. Cover the top hood, and let the sandwich cook for 5 minutes. 9. Rotate the handle of the cooking plate clockwise until it stops. 10. Lift the hood, the rings and transfer the sandwich to a plate. 11. Serve.

Serving Suggestion: Serve the sandwich with crispy fries on the side.

Variation Tip: Add a layer of sliced bell peppers for a change of taste.

Nutritional Information Per Serving: Calories 334 | Fat 16g |Sodium 462mg | Carbs 3g | Fiber 0.4g | Sugar 3g | Protein 35.3g

Egg, Anchovy and Ham Hamburgers

Prep time: 15 minutes | Cook Time: 20 minutes | Serves: 4

Ingredients:

1 large shallot, diced
1 garlic clove, minced
1½ teaspoon ground coriander
1½ teaspoon fresh ground fennel seeds
1 tablespoon light brown sugar
1 anchovy fillet
2 tablespoons lemon juice
10 ounces canned or boxed tomato purée

1 teaspoon dried oregano
1 teaspoon salt
black pepper, to taste
8 eggs, beaten
8 slices sharp cheddar cheese
8 slices bacon, cooked
4 hamburger buns, split in half

Preparation:

1. Sauté shallot and garlic with oil in a skillet for 3 minutes. 2. Stir in coriander, fennel seeds, brown sugar, anchovy fillet, lemon juice, tomato puree, oregano, black pepper and salt. 3. Mix well and cook for 7 minutes on low heat with occasional stirring. 4. Beat eggs with black pepper and salt in a bowl. 5. Preheat your Hamilton Beach Breakfast Sandwich Maker until PREHEAT light gets green. 6. Lift the top cover, ring, and cooking plate. 7. Place one bun inside the bottom tray of the sandwich maker. 8. Top it with ¼ of the tomato jam. 9. Now lower the cooking plate and top rings then pour in ¼ of the egg mixture. 10. Add a slice of cheddar cheese, bacon slice and another bun half on top. 11. Cover the top hood, and let the sandwich cook for 5 minutes. 12. Rotate the handle of the cooking plate clockwise until it stops. 13. Lift the hood, the rings and transfer the sandwich to a plate. 14. Repeat the same steps with the remaining ingredients. 15. Serve.

Serving Suggestion: Serve the sandwich with crispy bacon and your favorite sauce on the side.

Variation Tip: Add a layer of pickled veggies for a change of taste.

Nutritional Information Per Serving: Calories 405 | Fat 20g |Sodium 941mg | Carbs 6.1g | Fiber 0.9g | Sugar 0.9g | Protein 45.2g

Fried Egg, Tomato and Avocado Sandwich

Prep time: 15 minutes | Cook Time: 20 minutes | Serves: 4

Ingredients:

Avocado mixture
½ cup avocado, pitted, peeled
2 tablespoons chopped red onion

¼ teaspoon salt
⅛ teaspoon pepper

Sandwich
4 tablespoons butter, softened
4 large eggs
8 slices Italian bread, cut into 4 inches' round

8 slices ripe tomato
4 (¾-ounce) slices of provolone cheese

Preparation:

1. Beat eggs with butter in a suitable bowl and keep it aside. 2. Mash avocado in a bowl then add red onion, black pepper and salt and mix well. 3. Preheat your Hamilton Beach Breakfast Sandwich Maker until PREHEAT light gets green. 4. Lift the top cover, ring, and cooking plate. 5. Place one bread slice inside the bottom tray of the sandwich maker. 6. Spread ¼ of the avocado mixture on top. 7. Now lower the cooking plate and top rings then pour in ¼ egg. 8. Place a tomato and cheese slice and the other top half of the muffin on top. 9. Cover the top hood, and let the sandwich cook for 5 minutes. 10. Rotate the handle of the cooking plate clockwise until it stops. 11. Lift the hood, the rings and transfer the sandwich to a plate. 12. Repeat the same steps with the remaining ingredients. 13. Serve.

Serving Suggestion: Serve the sandwich with crispy carrot chips on the side.
Variation Tip: Add a layer of pickled veggies for a change of taste.
Nutritional Information Per Serving: Calories 440 | Fat 14g |Sodium 220mg | Carbs 2g | Fiber 0.2g | Sugar 1g | Protein 37g

Chapter 4 Fish and Seafood Recipes

39 Crispy Fish and Onion Sandwich

39 Tasty Cod Sandwich

39 Tartar Cod-Cucumber Sandwich

40 Homemade Tuna Burgers

40 Shrimp Salad Burgers

40 Blackened Salmon Sandwich

41 Lemon Shrimp and Cod Burgers

41 Salmon and Carrot Sandwich

42 Delicious Lobster Muffin Sandwiches

42 Tartar Cod and Slaw Sandwiches

43 Dill Shrimp Sandwich

43 Salmon Patty Sandwiches

43 Scallop Corn Bacon Burgers

44 Crispy Seafood Burger

44 Thai-Style Tuna & Cucumber Burgers

45 Lime Tuna Salad Sandwich

45 Tuna Olive Hamburgers

45 Mayo Tuna Cheeseburgers

46 Crispy Shrimp Avocado Burgers

46 Salmon Burgers with Harissa Mayo & Cumber Relish

Crispy Fish and Onion Sandwich

Prep Time: 15 minutes | Cook Time: 20 minutes | Serves: 2

Ingredients:

4 frozen breaded fish strips
Cooking oil
2 tablespoons mayonnaise

1 teaspoon sweet pickle relish
2 whole wheat burger buns, split in half
4 slices sweet onion

Preparation:

1. Spray fish strips with oil. 2. In a pan over medium heat, cook the fish until golden and crispy. 3. In a bowl, mix mayo, sweet pickle relish and onion. 4. Preheat the Breakfast Sandwich Maker until the green PREHEAT light comes on. Lift cover, top ring, and cooking plate. 5. Place half of the muffin in the bottom ring of the sandwich maker and add the ½ of the prepared fillings. 6. Lower the cooking plate and top ring. 7. Place another bun half in the cooking plate. 8. Close the cover and cook for 5 minutes. Rotate the cooking plate handle clockwise until it stops. Then lift the cover and rings and carefully remove the sandwich with plastic spatula. 9. Repeat the process for the remaining ingredients. 10. Serve.
Serving Suggestion: Serve the sandwich with your favorite sauce on the side.
Variation Tip: You can add a lettuce leave to the filling as well.
Nutritional Information Per Serving: Calories 551 | Fat 31g |Sodium 1329mg | Carbs 1.5g | Fiber 0.8g | Sugar 0.4g | Protein 64g

Tasty Cod Sandwich

Prep Time: 15 minutes | Cook Time: 10 minutes | Serves: 2

Ingredients:

4 whole wheat bread slices, cut in 4-inch circle
2 cod fillets, grilled and sliced into strips
4 tablespoons salsa

1 teaspoon sweet pickle relish
½ teaspoon dried parsley flakes

Preparation:

1. Preheat the Breakfast Sandwich Maker until the green PREHEAT light comes on. Lift cover, top ring, and cooking plate. 2. Place one bread slice in the bottom ring of the sandwich maker. 3. Spread ½ of the cod fillets, salsa and sweet pickle relish on top. 4. Sprinkle with parsley flakes. 5. Lower the cooking plate and top ring. 6. Top with the other circle of the bread. 7. Close the cover and cook for 5 minutes. Rotate the cooking plate handle clockwise until it stops. Then lift the cover and rings and carefully remove the sandwich with plastic spatula. 8. Repeat the process for the remaining ingredients. 9. Serve.
Serving Suggestion: Serve the sandwich with crispy bacon and your favorite sauce on the side.
Variation Tip: Add some additional dried herbs to the filling.
Nutritional Information Per Serving: Calories 410 | Fat 17.8g |Sodium 619mg | Carbs 21g | Fiber 1.4g | Sugar 1.8g | Protein 38.4g

Tartar Cod-Cucumber Sandwich

Prep Time: 15 minutes | Cook Time: 10 minutes | Serves: 2

Ingredients:

4 whole wheat bread slices, cut in 4-inch circle
4 slices cucumber

2 breaded cod fillets, cooked
4 tablespoons tartar sauce

Preparation:

1. Preheat the Breakfast Sandwich Maker until the green PREHEAT light comes on. Lift cover, top ring, and cooking plate. 2. Place one bread slice in the bottom ring of the sandwich maker. 3. Add ½ of the cucumber and cod fillets on top. 4. Drizzle with ½ of the tartar sauce. 5. Lower the cooking plate and top ring. 6. Top with the other circle of the bread. 7. Close the cover and cook for 5 minutes. Rotate the cooking plate handle clockwise until it stops. Then lift the cover and rings and carefully remove the sandwich with plastic spatula. 8. Repeat the same steps with the remaining ingredients. 9. Serve.
Serving Suggestion: Serve the sandwich with coleslaw and your favorite sauce on the side.
Variation Tip: You can add a drizzle of paprika on top of the filling as well.
Nutritional Information Per Serving: Calories 396 | Fat 23.2g |Sodium 622mg | Carbs 0.7g | Fiber 0g | Sugar 0g | Protein 45.6g

Homemade Tuna Burgers

Prep Time: 15 minutes | Cook Time: 25 minutes | Serves: 4

Ingredients:

For the Patty:
2 cups tuna flakes
1 egg, beaten
½ cup breadcrumbs
Sandwich
8 whole wheat bread slices, cut in 4-inch circle

1 red onion, minced
1 tablespoon celery, chopped

4 tablespoons mayonnaise

Preparation:

1. In a bowl, mix the patty ingredients and form the mixture into patties. 2. Cook the patties in a pan over medium heat for 2 to 3 minutes on each side. 3. Preheat the Breakfast Sandwich Maker until the green PREHEAT light comes on. Lift cover, top ring, and cooking plate. 4. Place one bread slice in the bottom ring of the sandwich maker and spread it with ¼ mayonnaise. 5. Lower the cooking plate and top ring; then add a patty. 6. Top with ¼ of the remaining fillings and the other circle of the bread. 7. Close the cover and cook for 5 minutes. Rotate the cooking plate handle clockwise until it stops. Then lift the cover and rings and carefully remove the sandwich with plastic spatula. 8. Repeat the same steps with the remaining ingredients. 9. Serve.

Serving Suggestion: Serve the sandwich with your favorite sauce on the side.

Variation Tip: Add some additional ground black pepper to the filling.

Nutritional Information Per Serving: Calories 437 | Fat 28g |Sodium 1221mg | Carbs 22.3g | Fiber 0.9g | Sugar 8g | Protein 30.3g

Shrimp Salad Burgers

Prep Time: 15 minutes | Cook Time: 10 minutes | Serves: 2

Ingredients:

1 cup shrimp, peeled, deveined, cooked and chopped
4 tablespoons mayonnaise
1 teaspoon lemon juice

1 tablespoon green onion, chopped
1 teaspoon Old Bay seasoning
2 burger buns, split

Preparation:

1. In a bowl, combine all the ingredients except the burger buns. 2. Preheat the Breakfast Sandwich Maker until the green PREHEAT light comes on. Lift cover, top ring, and cooking plate. 3. Add half of a burger bun in the bottom ring of the breakfast sandwich maker. 4. Then spread with ½ of the shrimp mixture. 5. Lower the cooking plate and top ring. 6. Top with the other bun half. 7. Close the cover and cook for 5 minutes. Rotate the cooking plate handle clockwise until it stops. Then lift the cover and rings and carefully remove the sandwich with plastic spatula. 8. Repeat the process for the remaining ingredients. 9. Serve.

Serving Suggestion: Serve the sandwich with crispy bacon and your favorite sauce on the side.

Variation Tip: You can add a lettuce leave to the filling as well.

Nutritional Information Per Serving: Calories 352 | Fat 9.1g |Sodium 1294mg | Carbs 3.9g | Fiber 1g | Sugar 1g | Protein 61g

Blackened Salmon Sandwich

Prep Time: 15 minutes | Cook Time: 16 minutes | Serves: 2

Ingredients:

2 salmon fillets
2 teaspoons blackening seasoning
4 whole bread slices, cut in 4-inch circle

4 tablespoons mayonnaise
1 red onion, sliced thinly

Preparation:

1. Preheat a grill to medium heat. 2. Sprinkle the salmon fillets with blackening seasoning and grill for 3 to 4 minutes per side. 3. Preheat the Breakfast Sandwich Maker until the green PREHEAT light comes on. Lift cover, top ring, and cooking plate. 4. Place on bread slice, cut-side up, in bottom ring of Breakfast Sandwich Maker. 5. Spread with half of the mayonnaise. 6. Add half of grilled salmon fillets and onion slices on top. 7. Lower the cooking plate and top ring. 8. Top with the other circle of the bread. 9. Close the cover and cook for 5 minutes. Rotate the cooking plate handle clockwise until it stops. Then lift the cover and rings and carefully remove the sandwich with plastic spatula. 10. Repeat the same steps with the remaining ingredients. 11. Serve.

Serving Suggestion: Serve the sandwich with your favorite sauce on the side.

Variation Tip: Add some additional dried herbs to the filling.

Nutritional Information Per Serving: Calories 374 | Fat 25g |Sodium 275mg | Carbs 7.3g | Fiber 0g | Sugar 6g | Protein 12.3g

Lemon Shrimp and Cod Burgers

Prep time: 15 minutes | Cook Time: 20 minutes | Serves: 4

Ingredients:

12 ounces medium shrimp, peeled, deveined, and cut into chunks
8 ounces cod, cut into chunks
¾ cup fresh breadcrumbs
¼ cup drained capers, rinsed
2 medium scallions, sliced
3 tablespoons chopped parsley

¼ cup lemon juice
1¼ teaspoons salt
¾ teaspoon black pepper
Vegetable oil, for brushing
4 large lettuce leaves
4 hamburger buns, split in half

Preparation:

1. In a food processor, blend shrimp, cod, crumbs, scallions, capers, lemon juice, parsley, black pepper and salt for 1 minute. 2. Form the mixture into 4 patties and sear them in a skillet greased with oil for 5 minutes on each side. 3. Preheat the Breakfast Sandwich Maker until the green PREHEAT light comes on. Lift cover, top ring, and cooking plate. 4. Place half of a bun, cut-side up, inside the bottom ring of the sandwich maker. 5. Lower the cooking plate and top ring. 6. Place a patty in the cooking plate, then top with a lettuce leaf and the other half of the bun. 7. Close the cover and cook for 5 minutes. Rotate the cooking plate handle clockwise until it stops. Then lift the cover and rings and carefully remove the sandwich with plastic spatula. 8. Repeat the process for the remaining ingredients. 9. Serve.
Serving Suggestion: Serve the sandwich with crispy fries on the side.
Variation Tip: Add a layer of spicy mayo and pickled veggies for a change of taste.
Nutritional Information Per Serving: Calories 325 | Fat 16g |Sodium 431mg | Carbs 2g | Fiber 1.2g | Sugar 4g | Protein 23g

Salmon and Carrot Sandwich

Prep Time: 15 minutes | Cook Time: 10 minutes | Serves: 2

Ingredients:

1 cup salmon flakes
¼ cup cream cheese
1 tablespoon mayonnaise
1 tablespoon lemon juice
2 tablespoons celery, minced

2 tablespoons carrot, shredded
1 teaspoon dill weed
Salt and black pepper to taste
2 burger buns, split in half

Preparation:

1. In a bowl, combine all the ingredients except the burger buns. 2. Preheat the Breakfast Sandwich Maker until the green PREHEAT light comes on. Lift cover, top ring, and cooking plate. 3. Place half of burger bun, cut-side up, in bottom ring of Breakfast Sandwich Maker. 4. Spread with ½ of the salmon mixture. 5. Lower the cooking plate and top ring. 6. Place the other top half of the bun in the cooking plate. 7. Close the cover and cook for 5 minutes. Rotate the cooking plate handle clockwise until it stops. Then lift the cover and rings and carefully remove the sandwich with plastic spatula. 8. Repeat the same steps with the remaining ingredients. 9. Serve.
Serving Suggestion: Serve the sandwich with coleslaw and your favorite sauce on the side.
Variation Tip: You can add a lettuce leave to the filling as well.
Nutritional Information Per Serving: Calories 310 | Fat 17g |Sodium 271mg | Carbs 4.3g | Fiber 0.9g | Sugar 2.1g | Protein 35g

Delicious Lobster Muffin Sandwiches

Prep time: 15 minutes | Cook Time: 5 minutes | Serves: 4

Ingredients:

1 tablespoon butter, softened
4 English muffins, split
4 large leaf (blank)s lettuce leaves
1 ½ lbs. cooked and cubed lobster meat
2 tablespoons mayonnaise
1 teaspoon fresh lime juice

1 dash hot pepper sauce
2 medium green onions, chopped
1 stalk celery, chopped
1 pinch salt and black pepper to taste
1 pinch dried basil

Preparation:

1. Mix lobster meat with butter, mayonnaise, lime juice, hot pepper sauce, green onion, black pepper, salt, basil and celery in a bowl. 2. Preheat your Hamilton Beach Breakfast Sandwich Maker until PREHEAT light gets green. 3. Lift the top cover, ring, and cooking plate. 4. Place half of the English muffin, cut-side up, inside the bottom tray of the sandwich maker. 5. Arrange a lettuce leaf on top of the English muffin, then add ¼ of the lobster mixture on top. 6. Now lower the cooking plate and top rings. 7. Place the other top half of the muffin on top. 8. Cover the top hood, and let the sandwich cook for 5 minutes. 9. Rotate the handle of the cooking plate clockwise until it stops. 10. Lift the hood, the rings and transfer the sandwich to a plate. 11. Repeat the same steps with the remaining ingredients. 12. Serve.

Serving Suggestion: Serve the sandwich with crispy carrot chips on the side.

Variation Tip: Add a layer of pickled onions for a change of taste.

Nutritional Information Per Serving: Calories 380 | Fat 20g |Sodium 686mg | Carbs 3g | Fiber 1g | Sugar 1.2g | Protein 21g

Tartar Cod and Slaw Sandwiches

Prep time: 15 minutes | Cook Time: 15 minutes | Serves: 4

Ingredients:

Slaw
1 small head cabbage, shredded
½ small red onion, sliced
Salt and black pepper, to taste
2 teaspoons cider vinegar

1 teaspoon Dijon mustard
3 tablespoons mayonnaise
1 tablespoon sugar

Tartar sauce
3 tablespoons mayonnaise
2 teaspoons sweet pickle relish
1 tablespoon capers, rinsed, drained, and chopped

1 teaspoon sugar
1 teaspoon Dijon mustard

Fish
2 quarts peanut oil
1 ½ cups all-purpose flour
½ cup cornstarch
Salt and black pepper, to taste
1 teaspoon baking powder

¼ teaspoon paprika
12 ounces cod filet, cut into four portions
1 cup light beer
4 burger buns, split in half

Preparation:

1. Mix all the slaw ingredients in a suitable bowl and keep it aside. 2. Whisk all the tartar sauce ingredients in another bowl and set it aside. 3. Mix flour with cornstarch, baking powder, black pepper, salt, paprika and beer in a bowl. 4. Set a deep frying pan with oil over medium-high heat. 5. Dip the fish in the beer batter, then deep fry until golden brown. 6. Transfer the fried fish to a plate lined with parchment paper. 7. Preheat your Hamilton Beach Breakfast Sandwich Maker until PREHEAT light gets green. 8. Lift the top cover, ring, and cooking plate. 9. Place half of a bun, cut-side up, inside the bottom tray of the sandwich maker. 10. Spread ¼ of the fish, slaw and tartar sauce on top. 11. Now lower the cooking plate and top rings. 12. Place the other top half of the bun on top. 13. Cover the top hood, and let the sandwich cook for 5 minutes. 14. Rotate the handle of the cooking plate clockwise until it stops. 15. Lift the hood, the rings and transfer the sandwich to a plate. 16. Repeat the same with the remaining ingredients. 17. Serve.

Serving Suggestion: Serve the sandwich with a cauliflower bacon salad on the side.

Variation Tip: Enjoy sautéed veggies on the side for a change of taste.

Nutritional Information Per Serving: Calories 391 | Fat 5g |Sodium 88mg | Carbs 3g | Fiber 0g | Sugar 0g | Protein 27g

Dill Shrimp Sandwich

Prep Time: 15 minutes | Cook Time: 20 minutes | Serves: 4

Ingredients:

1 cup shrimp, peeled, deveined, cooked and chopped
4 tablespoons mayonnaise
1 teaspoon lemon juice

1 teaspoon dried dill
4 burger buns

Preparation:

1. Combine all ingredients in a bowl except the buns. 2. Preheat the Breakfast Sandwich Maker until the green PREHEAT light comes on. Lift cover, top ring, and cooking plate. 3. Place half of the bun in the bottom ring of the sandwich maker and top with ¼th of the shrimp mixture. 4. Lower the cooking plate and top ring. 5. Place the other top half of the bun in the cooking plate. 6. Close the cover and cook for 5 minutes. Rotate the cooking plate handle clockwise until it stops. Then lift the cover and rings and carefully remove the sandwich with plastic spatula. 7. Repeat the same steps with the remaining ingredients. 8. Serve.
Serving Suggestion: Serve the sandwich with your favorite sauce on the side.
Variation Tip: Add some additional dried herbs to the filling.
Nutritional Information Per Serving: Calories 330| Fat 10.4 g |Sodium 690 mg | Carbs 11.4 g | Fiber 3 g | Sugar 4.7g | Protein 48 g

Salmon Patty Sandwiches

Prep time: 15 minutes | Cook Time: 20 minutes | Serves: 4

Ingredients:

4 salmon patties
1 crunch chopped salad kit

4 English muffins, split in half
8 ounces hill country fare chipotle mayo

Preparation:

1. Sear the salmon patties in a skillet for 5 minutes per side. 2. Preheat your Hamilton Beach Breakfast Sandwich Maker until PREHEAT light gets green. 3. Lift the top cover, ring, and cooking plate. 4. Place half of a muffin, cut-side up, inside the bottom tray of the sandwich maker. 5. Spread ¼ mayonnaise, a salmon patty and ¼ chopped salad on top. 6. Now lower the cooking plate and top rings. 7. Place the other top half of the muffin on top. 8. Cover the top hood, and let the burger cook for 5 minutes. 9. Rotate the handle of the cooking plate clockwise until it stops. 10. Lift the hood, the rings and transfer the burger to a plate. 11. Repeat the same steps with the remaining ingredients. 12. Serve.
Serving Suggestion: Serve the sandwich with a cauliflower bacon salad on the side.
Variation Tip: Add a layer of sliced bell peppers for a change of taste.
Nutritional Information Per Serving: Calories 361 | Fat 16g |Sodium 515mg | Carbs 29.3g | Fiber 0.1g | Sugar 18.2g | Protein 33.3g

Scallop Corn Bacon Burgers

Prep time: 15 minutes | Cook Time: 30 minutes | Serves: 6

Ingredients:

½ cup mayonnaise
3 tablespoons ketchup
1 teaspoon Tabasco sauce
Salt and black pepper, to taste
3 ears of corn, shucked

1 ½ lbs. sea scallops, chopped
6 soft hamburger buns, split
6 lettuce leaves
6 thick tomato slices
12 slices cooked thick-cut bacon

Preparation:

1. In a bowl, toss the scallops with corn, tabasco sauce, black pepper, ketchup and mayonnaise. 2. Preheat the Breakfast Sandwich Maker until the green PREHEAT light comes on. Lift cover, top ring, and cooking plate. 3. Place half of a bun, cut-side up, inside the bottom ring of the sandwich maker. 4. Top with ⅙ of the scallop mixture, 1 lettuce leaf, a tomato slice and 2 bacon slices. 5. Lower the cooking plate and top ring. 6. Place the other top half of the bun in the cooking plate. 7. Close the cover and cook for 5 minutes. Rotate the cooking plate handle clockwise until it stops. Then lift the cover and rings and carefully remove the sandwich with plastic spatula. 8. Repeat the same steps with the remaining ingredients. 9. Serve.
Serving Suggestion: Serve the sandwich with crispy fries on the side.
Variation Tip: Add a layer of pickled veggies for a change of taste.
Nutritional Information Per Serving: Calories 282 | Fat 15g |Sodium 526mg | Carbs 20g | Fiber 0.6g | Sugar 3.3g | Protein 16g

Crispy Seafood Burger

Prep time: 15 minutes | Cook Time: 11 minutes | Serves: 4

Ingredients:

½ lb. prawns
½ lb. scallops
½ lb. skinless halibut
2 green onions, chopped
2 tablespoons fresh parsley, chopped
2 tablespoons dill, chopped
1 tablespoon lemon zest
Juice from half a lemon

Salt and black pepper, to taste
3 eggs
½ cup panko breadcrumbs
½ red chili
3 tablespoons butter
3 tablespoons neutral oil
4 burger buns, cut in half

Preparation:

1. Blend prawns, scallops, halibut, green onions, parsley, dill, lemon zest, lemon juice, red chili, salt and black pepper in a food processor. 2. Make 4 patties out of this seafood mixture. 3. Beat eggs with black pepper and salt then dip patties in them. 4. Coat the patties with the panko breadcrumbs. 5. Set a pan with oil and butter on medium-high heat. 6. Sear the patties in the hot oil for 3 minutes per side. 7. Preheat your Hamilton Beach Breakfast Sandwich Maker until PREHEAT light gets green. 8. Lift the top cover, ring, and cooking plate. 9. Place half of a bun, cut-side up, inside the bottom tray of the sandwich maker. 10. Place a seafood patty on top. 11. Now lower the cooking plate and top rings. 12. Place the other top half of the muffin on top. 13. Cover the top hood, and let the sandwich cook for 5 minutes. 14. Rotate the handle of the cooking plate clockwise until it stops. 15. Lift the hood, the rings and transfer the sandwich to a plate. 16. Repeat the same steps with the remaining ingredients. 17. Serve.

Serving Suggestion: Serve the sandwich with crispy sweet potato fries on the side.

Variation Tip: you can add a lettuce leaf to the filling as well.

Nutritional Information Per Serving: Calories 425 | Fat 15g | Sodium 345mg | Carbs 2.3g | Fiber 1.4g | Sugar 3g | Protein 23.3g

Thai-Style Tuna & Cucumber Burgers

Prep time: 15 minutes | Cook Time: 26 minutes | Serves: 4

Ingredients:

2 Kirby cucumbers, sliced
¼ medium red onion, sliced
3 tablespoons rice vinegar
1 teaspoon sugar
Salt and black pepper, to taste
2 teaspoons fresh ginger, grated
1 garlic clove, smashed
1 Thai or serrano chile, seeded and minced

2 tablespoons Asian fish sauce
2 tablespoons cilantro, chopped
1 tablespoon basil, chopped
1½ lbs. sushi-quality tuna
1½ tablespoon vegetable oil
1½ teaspoon Asian sesame oil
4 hamburger buns, split in half
2 tablespoons chopped dry-roasted peanuts

Preparation:

1. Blend tuna with basil, cilantro, fish sauce, serrano chile, garlic, ginger, black pepper, sugar, salt, rice vinegar and red onion in a bowl. 2. Make 4 tuna patties out of this mixture and sear them in a pan greased with oil for 3 minutes per side. 3. Preheat your Hamilton Beach Breakfast Sandwich Maker until PREHEAT light gets green. 4. Lift the top cover, ring, and cooking plate. 5. Place half of a bun, cut-side up, inside the bottom tray of the sandwich maker. 6. Arrange a seared tuna patty and ¼ of peanuts and cucumbers on top. 7. Now lower the cooking plate and top rings. 8. Place the other top half of the bun on top. 9. Cover the top hood, and let the sandwich cook for 5 minutes. 10. Rotate the handle of the cooking plate clockwise until it stops. 11. Lift the hood, the rings and transfer the sandwich to a plate. 12. Repeat the same steps with the remaining ingredients. 13. Serve.

Serving Suggestion: Serve the sandwich with a broccoli salad on the side.

Variation Tip: you can add a lettuce leaf to the filling as well.

Nutritional Information Per Serving: Calories 392 | Fat 16g | Sodium 466mg | Carbs 23.9g | Fiber 0.9g | Sugar 0.6g | Protein 48g

Lime Tuna Salad Sandwich

Prep Time: 15 minutes | Cook Time: 5 minutes | Serves: 2

Ingredients:

1 cup tuna flakes
4 tablespoons mayonnaise
1 tablespoon capers
1 teaspoon lime juice

1 teaspoon tarragon
¼ teaspoon lemon pepper seasoning
2 burger buns, split

Preparation:

1. Mix all ingredients except buns. 2. Preheat your Hamilton Beach Breakfast Sandwich Maker. 3. Lift the top cover, ring, and cooking plate. 4. Place the lower half of the muffin in the sandwich maker. 5. Add one burger bun (bottom) inside. 6. Top with ½ of the tuna mixture. 7. Now lower the cooking plate and top rings. 8. Place the other top half of the bun on top. 9. Cover the top hood, and let the sandwich cook for 5 minutes. 10. When finished cooking, rotate the handle of the cooking plate clockwise until it stops. 11. Lift the hood, the rings and transfer the sandwich to a plate. 12. Repeat the same steps with the remaining ingredients. 13. Serve.

Serving Suggestion: Serve the sandwich with your favorite sauce on the side.

Variation Tip: You can add a layer of your favorite sauce to the filling as well.

Nutritional Information Per Serving: Calories 326 | Fat 13.4g |Sodium 315mg | Carbs 36.8g | Fiber 5.6g | Sugar 3.7g | Protein 15.9g

Tuna Olive Hamburgers

Prep time: 15 minutes | Cook Time: 5 minutes | Serves: 4

Ingredients:

1¼ lbs. fresh tuna, diced
2 scallions, sliced
12 pitted Kalamata olives, coarsely chopped
1 tablespoon salted capers, rinsed and minced
Salt and black pepper, to taste

Olive oil, for brushing
¼ cup mayonnaise
1½ teaspoon anchovy paste
4 brioche buns, split

Preparation:

1. Mix tuna meat with scallions, olives, and capers in a bowl. 2. Preheat your Hamilton Beach Breakfast Sandwich Maker until PREHEAT light gets green. 3. Lift the top cover, ring, and cooking plate. 4. Place half of a bun, cut-side up, inside the bottom tray of the sandwich maker. 5. Add ¼ of mayo, anchovy paste and tuna mixture on top. 6. Place the other top half of the bun on top. 7. Lower the top plate and ring. 8. Cover the top hood, and let the sandwich cook for 5 minutes. 9. Rotate the handle of the cooking plate clockwise until it stops. 10. Lift the hood, the rings and transfer the sandwich to a plate. 11. Repeat the same steps with the remaining ingredients. 12. Serve.

Serving Suggestion: Serve the sandwich with crispy carrot chips on the side.

Variation Tip: Add a layer of spicy mayo and pickled veggies for a change of taste.

Nutritional Information Per Serving: Calories 309 | Fat 25g |Sodium 463mg | Carbs 19.9g | Fiber 0.3g | Sugar 0.3g | Protein 18g

Mayo Tuna Cheeseburgers

Prep Time: 15 minutes | Cook Time: 5 minutes | Serves: 2

Ingredients:

1 cup tuna flakes
4 tablespoons mayonnaise
1 tablespoon celery, minced

1 tablespoon green onion, minced
2 burger buns, split
2 mozzarella Cheese, slices

Preparation:

1. Mix all ingredients except buns and cheese. 2. Preheat your Hamilton Beach Breakfast Sandwich Maker. 3. Lift the top cover, ring, and cooking plate. 4. Add one burger bun inside. 5. Spread with ½ of the tuna mixture. 6. Top with ½ of the cheese. 7. Now lower the cooking plate and top rings. 8. Place the other top half of the bun on top. 9. Cover the top hood, and let the sandwich cook for 5 minutes. 10. When finished cooking, rotate the handle of the cooking plate clockwise until it stops. 11. Lift the hood, the rings and transfer the sandwich to a plate. 12. Repeat the same steps with the remaining ingredients. 13. Serve.

Serving Suggestion: Serve the sandwich with crispy bacon and your favorite sauce on the side.

Variation Tip: Add some additional ground black pepper to the filling.

Nutritional Information Per Serving: Calories 459 | Fat 17.7g |Sodium 1516mg | Carbs 1.7g | Fiber 0.5g | Sugar 0.4g | Protein 69.2g

Crispy Shrimp Avocado Burgers

Prep time: 15 minutes | Cook Time: 11 minutes | Serves: 4

Ingredients:

5 tablespoons unsalted butter
1 lb. peeled and deveined large shrimp, chopped
1 large egg
¾ cup panko
¼ cup scallions, chopped
1½ teaspoon salt
¾ teaspoon old bay seasoning
½ teaspoon lemon zest

1½ tablespoon fresh lemon juice
½ cup mayonnaise
1 tablespoon whole-grain mustard
1 teaspoon Mexican-style hot sauce
4 sesame seed hamburger buns, split
1 cup shredded iceberg lettuce
1 small tomato, sliced
1 ripe medium-size avocado, sliced

Preparation:

1. Mix mayonnaise with salt, mustard, hot sauce, old bay seasoning and scallion in a bowl. 2. Dip the shrimp in the egg then in panko crumbs. 3. Melt butter in a skillet and sear the shrimp for 2-3 minutes per side until golden brown. 4. Fry all the coated shrimp and transfer them to a plate. 5. Preheat your Hamilton Beach Breakfast Sandwich Maker until PREHEAT light gets green. 6. Lift the top cover, ring, and cooking plate. 7. Place half of a bun, cut-side up, inside the bottom tray of the sandwich maker. 8. Arrange a lettuce leaf on top of the bun then add ¼ of the mayonnaise on top. 9. Now lower the cooking plate and top rings, place ¼ of the shrimp, tomato, avocado and lettuce on top. 10. Place the other top half of the bun on top. 11. Cover the top hood, and let the sandwich cook for 5 minutes. 12. Rotate the handle of the cooking plate clockwise until it stops. 13. Lift the hood, the rings and transfer the sandwich to a plate. 14. Repeat the same steps with the remaining ingredients. 15. Serve.
Serving Suggestion: Serve the sandwich with crispy zucchini fries on the side.
Variation Tip: Add a layer of pickled veggies for a change of taste.
Nutritional Information Per Serving: Calories 305 | Fat 25g |Sodium 532mg | Carbs 2.3g | Fiber 0.4g | Sugar 2g | Protein 18.3g

Salmon Burgers with Harissa Mayo & Cumber Relish

Prep time: 15 minutes | Cook Time: 11 minutes | Serves: 6

Ingredients:

Cumber relish
1 English cucumber, sliced
⅓ cup rice vinegar
1 tablespoon chopped dill
Harissa mayo
⅔ cup mayonnaise
¼ cup Greek yoghurt
2 tablespoons harissa
1 teaspoon grated lemon zest
1 tablespoon fresh lemon juice
Kosher salt, to taste
Black pepper, to taste
Salmon burgers
To cook:
2 tablespoons unsalted butter
¼ cup olive oil

1 shallot, minced
1 teaspoon sugar
1 teaspoon kosher salt

5 scallions, chopped
1 small red bell pepper, chopped
1 small green bell pepper, chopped
1½ lbs. skinless center-cut salmon fillet, cut into cubes
½ cup plain dry breadcrumbs
1 tablespoon kosher salt
½ teaspoon black pepper

6 brioche buns, split
Lettuce and tomato slices, for serving

Preparation:

1. Blend all the ingredients for salmon burgers in a food processor for 1 minute. 2. Mix harissa mayo ingredients in a suitable bowl. 3. Whisk the cucumber relish ingredients in another bowl. 4. Set a pan with oil over medium heat. 5. Make 6 patties out of the salmon mixture and sear them in the oil for 3 minutes per side. 6. Preheat your Hamilton Beach Breakfast Sandwich Maker until PREHEAT light gets green. 7. Lift the top cover, ring, and cooking plate. 8. Place half of a bun cut-side up, inside the bottom tray of the sandwich maker. 9. Add ⅙ of the harissa mayo, 1 salmon patty and ⅙ of the cucumber relish on top. 10. Now lower the cooking plate and top rings. 11. Place the other top half of the bun on top. 12. Cover the top hood, and let the sandwich cook for 5 minutes. 13. Rotate the handle of the cooking plate clockwise until it stops. 14. Lift the hood, the rings and transfer the sandwich to a plate. 15. Repeat the same steps with the remaining ingredients. 16. Serve with the lettuce and tomato slices.
Serving Suggestion: Serve the sandwich with crispy bacon and your favorite sauce on the side.
Variation Tip: Add a layer of pickled onions for a change of taste.
Nutritional Information Per Serving: Calories 425 | Fat 14g |Sodium 411mg | Carbs 24g | Fiber 0.3g | Sugar 1g | Protein 28.3g

Chapter 5 Poultry Breakfast Sandwiches and Burgers

48 Turkey and Water Chestnut Burger

48 Grilled Chicken and Black Bean Sandwich

48 Cajun Chicken Sandwich

49 Cheese Chicken and Avocado Sandwich

49 Yogurt Chicken and Cheery Sandwich

49 Lemony Chicken Salad Sandwich

50 Cheese Chicken Patty Sandwich

50 Basil Chicken Pizza Burgers

50 Turkey Tomato Burgers

51 Tzatziki Turkey Burgers

51 Spinach and Chicken Mushroom Burgers

52 Cheese Turkey and Sauerkraut Sandwich

52 Chicken and Broccoli Sandwich

52 Sweet & Spicy Chicken Sandwich

53 Turkey and Mushroom Sandwich

53 Spicy Curried Turkey Burgers

53 Chicken and Red Cabbage Sandwich

54 Smoked Turkey and Cucumber Sandwich

54 Chicken, Green Chiles and Avocado Pita Sandwich

55 Honey-Mustard Turkey Burgers

55 Chipotle Turkey-Avocado Sliders

56 Herbed Chicken and Bacon Burgers

56 Herbed Turkey and Cranberry Burgers

57 Chili Turkey and Cilantro Burgers

57 Cheese Turkey Mushroom Burgers

Turkey and Water Chestnut Burger

Prep Time: 15 minutes | Cook Time: 10 minutes | Serves: 2

Ingredients:

1 egg
1 tablespoon of teriyaki sauce
1 teaspoon of fresh ginger, grated
1 tablespoon of water chestnut, chopped
1 tablespoon of dried breadcrumbs

Shredded lettuce
1 tablespoon of French fried onions
½ pound of pre-cooked turkey
1 teaspoon of frank's red hot sauce
2 sandwich buns, split

Preparation:

1. In a bowl, mix turkey, breadcrumbs, water chestnut, egg, ginger and teriyaki sauce. Form this mixture into 2 patties. 2. Preheat the Breakfast Sandwich Maker until the green PREHEAT light comes on. Lift cover, top ring, and cooking plate. 3. Place half of a bun in the bottom ring of the sandwich maker. 4. Lower the cooking plate and top ring. Place a patty in the cooking plate and spread half of the onions, lettuce and hot sauce. 5. Top with the other half of the bun. 6. Close the cover and cook for 5 minutes. Rotate the cooking plate handle clockwise until it stops. Then lift the cover and rings and carefully remove the sandwich with plastic spatula. 7. Repeat the same steps with the remaining ingredients. 8. Serve.

Serving Suggestion: Serve the sandwich with crispy bacon and your favorite sauce on the side.

Variation Tip: You can add a drizzle of paprika on top of the filling as well.

Nutritional Information Per Serving: Calories 350| Fat 19g |Sodium 168mg | Carbs 38g | Fiber 6g | Sugar 18.8g | | Protein 10g

Grilled Chicken and Black Bean Sandwich

Prep Time: 15 minutes | Cook Time: 10 minutes | Serves: 2

Ingredients:

1 cup of shredded lettuce
1 ripe avocado
1 sliced tomato
Black pepper and salt

¼ cup of jalapeno pepper, sliced
8 ounces of grilled chicken breast
⅔ cup of black beans, mashed
2 sandwich buns, split

Preparation:

1. Preheat the Breakfast Sandwich Maker until the green PREHEAT light comes on. Lift cover, top ring, and cooking plate. 2. Place half of a bun in the bottom ring of the sandwich maker. 3. Lower the cooking plate and top ring. Add ½ of the fillings to the cooking plate. 4. Top with the other half of the bun. 5. Close the cover and cook for 5 minutes. Rotate the cooking plate handle clockwise until it stops. Then lift the cover and rings and carefully remove the sandwich with plastic spatula. 6. Repeat the same steps with the remaining ingredients. 7. Serve.

Serving Suggestion: Serve the sandwich with coleslaw and your favorite sauce on the side.

Variation Tip: Add some additional ground black pepper to the filling.

Nutritional Information Per Serving: Calories 521 | Fat 17.1 g | Sodium 840mg | Carbs 65.5 g | Fiber 2.9 g | Sugar 2.6 g | Protein 26.1g

Cajun Chicken Sandwich

Prep Time: 15 minutes | Cook Time: 5 minutes | Serves: 1

Ingredients:

3 ounces of pre-cooked skinless chicken
Butter
Lettuce

1 split toasted buns
Onion
1½ tablespoons of Cajun seasoning

Preparation:

1. Rub inside and outside of the chicken with Cajun seasoning. 2. Preheat the Breakfast Sandwich Maker until the green PREHEAT light comes on. Lift cover, top ring, and cooking plate. 3. Place half of a bun in the bottom ring of the sandwich maker. Brush the top with butter. 4. Lower the cooking plate and top ring. Add the chicken and remaining fillings to the cooking plate. 5. Top with the other top half of the bun. 6. Close the cover and cook for 5 minutes. Rotate the cooking plate handle clockwise until it stops. Then lift the cover and rings and carefully remove the sandwich with plastic spatula. 7. Serve.

Serving Suggestion: Serve the sandwich with your favorite sauce on the side.

Variation Tip: You can add a lettuce leave to the filling as well.

Nutritional Information Per Serving: Calories 347| Fat 22.3g |Sodium 207mg | Carbs 1.6g | Fiber 0.3g | Sugar 0.5g| Protein 32.8g

Cheese Chicken and Avocado Sandwich

Prep Time: 15 minutes | Cook Time: 5 minutes | Serves: 1

Ingredients:

- 2 ounces of grilled boneless chicken breast
- 1 avocado
- 2 pieces of fried crisp bacon
- 1 tablespoon of mayonnaise
- 2 crisp lettuce leaves
- 1 ounce of blue cheese
- 1 ounce of cream cheese
- 1 bun, split

Preparation:

1. Preheat the Breakfast Sandwich Maker until the green PREHEAT light comes on. Lift cover, top ring, and cooking plate. 2. Place half of a bun in the bottom ring of the sandwich maker. 3. Lower the cooking plate and top ring. Add all the fillings to the cooking plate. 4. Top with the other half of the bun. 5. Close the cover and cook for 5 minutes. Rotate the cooking plate handle clockwise until it stops. Then lift the cover and rings and carefully remove the sandwich with plastic spatula. 6. Serve.

Serving Suggestion: Serve the sandwich with crispy bacon and your favorite sauce on the side.

Variation Tip: Add some additional dried herbs to the filling.

Nutritional Information Per Serving: Calories 310| Fat 6.9g |Sodium 296mg | Carbs 18.7g | Fiber 0.3g | Sugar 1.5g| Protein 30.2g

Yogurt Chicken and Cheery Sandwich

Prep Time: 15 minutes | Cook Time: 5 minutes | Serves: 1

Ingredients:

- 1 teaspoon of lemon juice
- 1 green onion
- Lettuce leaves
- 2 teaspoons of mayonnaise
- 2 tablespoons of dried tart cherries
- 1 croissant split
- Black pepper
- 1 cup of cooked chicken
- ⅛ cup of plain yogurt
- 1 teaspoon of chopped parsley

Preparation:

1. In a bowl, mix lemon juice, black pepper, mayonnaise, and yogurt. 2. Preheat the Breakfast Sandwich Maker until the green PREHEAT light comes on. Lift cover, top ring, and cooking plate. 3. Place half of a croissant in the bottom ring of the sandwich maker. 4. Lower the cooking plate and top ring. Add the remaining fillings to the cooking plate and spread the yogurt mixture on top. 5. Top with the other half of the croissant. 6. Close the cover and cook for 5 minutes. Rotate the cooking plate handle clockwise until it stops. Then lift the cover and rings and carefully remove the sandwich with plastic spatula. 7. Serve.

Serving Suggestion: Serve the sandwich with your favorite sauce on the side.

Variation Tip: You can add a lettuce leave to the filling as well.

Nutritional Information Per Serving: Calories 524| Fat 24 g |Sodium 568 mg | Carbs 24 g | Fiber 9 g | Sugar 5.2g | Protein 24 g

Lemony Chicken Salad Sandwich

Prep Time: 15 minutes | Cook Time: 5 minutes | Serves: 1

Ingredients:

- 1 teaspoon of lemon juice
- 2 multigrain bread, cut in 4-inch circle
- 1 tablespoon of mayonnaise
- 2 pound of chicken breast
- 1 teaspoon of fresh dill
- 2 lettuce leaves
- ⅛ teaspoons of salt
- 1 tablespoon of plain yogurt
- ⅛ teaspoons of grated lemon zest

Preparation:

1. In a bowl, mix dill, lemon juice, salt, yogurt, mayonnaise, and lemon zest. 2. Preheat the Breakfast Sandwich Maker until the green PREHEAT light comes on. Lift cover, top ring, and cooking plate. 3. Place one bread round in the bottom ring of the sandwich maker. 4. Lower the cooking plate and top ring. Add the lettuce leaves, chicken and sauce on top. 5. Then top with the other circle of the bread. 6. Close the cover and cook for 5 minutes. Rotate the cooking plate handle clockwise until it stops. Then lift the cover and rings and carefully remove the sandwich with plastic spatula. 7. Serve.

Serving Suggestion: Serve the sandwich with your favorite sauce on the side.

Variation Tip: Add some additional dried herbs to the filling.

Nutritional Information Per Serving: Calories 340 | Fat 15.5g | Sodium 404mg | Carbs 18.3g | Fiber 2g | Sugar 2.7g | Protein 30.9g

Cheese Chicken Patty Sandwich

Prep Time: 15 minutes | Cook Time: 5 minutes | Serves: 1

Ingredients:

1 ounce of chicken patties, cooked
1 split buns
1 sliced tomato
1 slice of Swiss cheese

Mustard
1 slice of ham
lettuce

Preparation:

1. Preheat the Breakfast Sandwich Maker until the green PREHEAT light comes on. Lift cover, top ring, and cooking plate. 2. Place half of the bun in the bottom ring of the sandwich maker. 3. Lower the cooking plate and top ring. Add the chicken patties and all the fillings to the cooking plate. 4. Top with the other half of the bun. 5. Close the cover and cook for 5 minutes. Rotate the cooking plate handle clockwise until it stops. Then lift the cover and rings and carefully remove the sandwich with plastic spatula. 6. Serve.

Serving Suggestion: Serve the sandwich with coleslaw and your favorite sauce on the side.

Variation Tip: Add some additional ground black pepper to the filling.

Nutritional Information Per Serving: Calories 386 | Fat 17g | Sodium 525mg | Carbs 36.1g | Fiber 2.6g | Sugar 2.2g | Protein 21g

Basil Chicken Pizza Burgers

Prep Time: 15 minutes | Cook Time: 10 minutes | Serves: 2

Ingredients:

2 buns, split
½ teaspoon of basil
4 ounces of ground chicken

2 slices of provolone cheese
1 cup of pizza sauce

Preparation:

1. Preheat the Breakfast Sandwich Maker until the green PREHEAT light comes on. Lift cover, top ring, and cooking plate. 2. Place half of a bun in the bottom ring of the sandwich maker. Top with 1 slice of provolone cheese, dried basil, and pizza sauce. 3. Lower the cooking plate and top ring, then add ½ of the ground chicken to the cooking plate. 4. Top with the other top half of the bun. 5. Close the cover and cook for 5 minutes. Rotate the cooking plate handle clockwise until it stops. Then lift the cover and rings and carefully remove the sandwich with plastic spatula. 6. Repeat the same steps with the remaining ingredients. 7. Serve.

Serving Suggestion: Serve the sandwich with crispy bacon and your favorite sauce on the side.

Variation Tip: You can add a drizzle of lemon juice on top of the filling as well.

Nutritional Information Per Serving: Calories 327 | Fat 18.3g | Sodium 512mg | Carbs 4.2g | Fiber 0.5g | Sugar 0.3g | Protein 35.3g

Turkey Tomato Burgers

Prep time: 15 minutes | Cook Time: 30 minutes | Serves: 6

Ingredients:

1 lb. ground turkey
1 large egg, beaten
2 garlic cloves, minced
1 tablespoon Worcestershire sauce
2 tablespoons parsley, chopped
Kosher salt, to taste

Black pepper, to taste
1 tablespoon olive oil
6 Hamburger buns, cut in half
6 Lettuce leaves
6 tomato slices
6 teaspoon Mayonnaise

Preparation:

1. In a food processor, blend turkey, egg, parsley, garlic, Worcestershire sauce, black pepper, and salt for 1 minute. Form this mixture into six equal-sized patties. 2. In a skillet over medium-high heat, warm the olive oil. 3. Sear the turkey patties in the oil for 5 minutes on each side. 4. Preheat the Breakfast Sandwich Maker until the green PREHEAT light comes on. Lift cover, top ring, and cooking plate. 5. Place half of a bun, cut-side up, inside the bottom ring of the sandwich maker. 6. Lower the cooking plate and top ring. Place a patty, a lettuce leaf, and a tomato slice in the cooking plate. Spread with 1 teaspoon mayonnaise. 7. Top with the other half of the bun. 8. Close the cover and cook for 5 minutes. Rotate the cooking plate handle clockwise until it stops. Then lift the cover and rings and carefully remove the sandwich with plastic spatula. 9. Repeat the same steps with the remaining ingredients. 10. Serve.

Serving Suggestion: Serve the sandwich with crispy zucchini fries on the side.

Variation Tip: you can add a lettuce leaf to the filling as well.

Nutritional Information Per Serving: Calories 448 | Fat 13g | Sodium 353mg | Carbs 23g | Fiber 0.4g | Sugar 1g | Protein 29g

Tzatziki Turkey Burgers

Prep time: 15 minutes | Cook Time: 20 minutes | Serves: 6

Ingredients:

2 lbs. ground turkey
2 teaspoons oregano
4 garlic cloves, minced
1 small onion, grated
¼ cup parsley, chopped
Tzatziki sauce
1 cup Greek yoghurt
½ English cucumber, grated
1 tablespoon dried dill or 2 tablespoons fresh dill
2 teaspoons za'atar, optional
Burger
6 romaine lettuce leaves
2 tomatoes, sliced

1 teaspoon cumin
1 teaspoon black pepper
2 teaspoons salt
2 tablespoons olive oil

1-2 garlic cloves, minced
½ teaspoons salt
¼ teaspoons pepper

4 ounces feta, crumbled
6 hamburger buns, toasted

Preparation:

1. In a bowl, mix all the Tzatziki sauce ingredients and set aside. 2. In a food processor, blend turkey with onion, oregano, garlic, cumin, parsley, black pepper, and salt for 1 minute. Form this mixture into six equal-sized patties. 3. Heat the olive oil in a skillet over medium-high heat. 4. Sear the turkey patties in the oil for 5 minutes on each side. 5. Preheat the Breakfast Sandwich Maker until the green PREHEAT light comes on. Lift cover, top ring, and cooking plate. 6. Place half of a bun, cut-side up, inside the bottom ring of the sandwich maker. 7. Lower the cooking plate and top ring. Place a patty, a lettuce leaf, a tomato slice, ⅙ feta and Tzatziki sauce in the cooking plate. 8. Top with the other half of the bun. 9. Close the cover and cook for 5 minutes. Rotate the cooking plate handle clockwise until it stops. Then lift the cover and rings and carefully remove the sandwich with plastic spatula. 10. Repeat the same steps with the remaining ingredients. 11. Serve.

Serving Suggestion: Serve the sandwich with crispy fries on the side.

Variation Tip: Add a layer of sliced bell peppers for a change of taste.

Nutritional Information Per Serving: Calories 345 | Fat 36g |Sodium 272mg | Carbs 41g | Fiber 0.2g | Sugar 0.1g | Protein 22.5g

Spinach and Chicken Mushroom Burgers

Prep time: 15 minutes | Cook Time: 40 minutes | Serves: 8

Ingredients:

1 lb. ground chicken
1 cup chopped spinach
⅓ cup Kalamata olives, chopped
1 ½ teaspoon lemon zest
½ teaspoon dried oregano
1 teaspoon garlic powder
¾ teaspoon salt

½ teaspoon black pepper
2 tablespoons olive oil
8 large Portobello mushrooms, cut in half horizontally
4 tablespoons Tzatziki
1 cup arugula
8 (¼ inch thick) rings red onion

Preparation:

1. In a food processor, blend chicken with spinach, olives, zest, oregano, garlic powder, salt, and black pepper for 1 minute. Form this mixture into 8 equal-sized patties. 2. Heat the olive oil in a skillet over medium-high heat. 3. Sear the chicken patties in the oil for 5 minutes on each side. 4. Preheat the Breakfast Sandwich Maker until the green PREHEAT light comes on. Lift cover, top ring, and cooking plate. 5. Place half of a Portobello mushroom, cut-side up, inside the bottom ring of the sandwich maker. 6. Lower the cooking plate and top ring. Place a patty, an onion ring, ⅛ of the Tzatziki and arugula in the cooking plate. 7. Top with the other half of the Portobello mushroom. 8. Close the cover and cook for 5 minutes. Rotate the cooking plate handle clockwise until it stops. Then lift the cover and rings and carefully remove the sandwich with plastic spatula. 9. Repeat the same steps with the remaining ingredients. 10. Serve.

Serving Suggestion: Serve the sandwich with a cauliflower bacon salad on the side.

Variation Tip: Add a layer of spicy mayo and pickled veggies for a change of taste.

Nutritional Information Per Serving: Calorics 395 | Fat 9.5g |Sodium 655mg | Carbs 34g | Fiber 0.4g | Sugar 0.4g | Protein 28.3g

Cheese Turkey and Sauerkraut Sandwich

Prep Time: 15 minutes | Cook Time: 10 minutes | Serves: 2

Ingredients:

4 ounces of turkey breast
1 tablespoon butter
4 dark rye bread slices, cut in 4-inch circle

4 ounces of sauerkraut
4 slices of Swiss cheese
Salad dressing

Preparation:

1. Preheat the Breakfast Sandwich Maker until the green PREHEAT light comes on. Lift cover, top ring, and cooking plate. 2. Place one bread round in the bottom ring of the sandwich maker. Brush the top with butter. 3. Lower the cooking plate and top ring. Add ½ of the turkey breast to the cooking plate. Add the Swiss cheese, sauerkraut, and salad dressing on top. 4. Then top with the other circle of the bread. 5. Close the cover and cook for 5 minutes. Rotate the cooking plate handle clockwise until it stops. Then lift the cover and rings and carefully remove the sandwich with plastic spatula. 6. Repeat the same steps with the remaining ingredients. 7. Serve.

Serving Suggestion: Serve the sandwich with your favorite sauce on the side.

Variation Tip: Add some additional dried herbs to the filling.

Nutritional Information Per Serving: Calories 565| Fat 30 g | Sodium 651mg | Carbs 20.3 g | Fiber1.4g | Sugar 1.7 g | Protein 53.1 g

Chicken and Broccoll Sandwich

Prep Time: 15 minutes | Cook Time: 5 minutes | Serves: 1

Ingredients:

1 teaspoon of Worcestershire sauce
1 package of grilled chicken breast
2 tablespoons of shredded Swiss cheese
1 can of condensed cream of mushroom soup

2 tablespoons of broccoli florets
2 white bread slices, cut in 4-inch circle
1 tablespoon of milk

Preparation:

1. Mix broccoli floret, mushroom soup, Swiss cheese, milk in a bowl. 2. Preheat your Hamilton Beach Breakfast Sandwich Maker. 3. Lift the top cover, ring, and cooking plate. 4. Place one bread slice in the sandwich maker. 5. Now lower the cooking plate and top rings, then add the broccoli floret mix on top. 6. Add the other circle of the bread on top. 7. Cover the top hood, and let the sandwich cook for 5 minutes. 8. When finished cooking, rotate the handle of the cooking plate clockwise until it stops. 9. Lift the hood, the rings and transfer the sandwich to a plate. 10. Serve.

Serving Suggestion: Serve the sandwich with coleslaw and your favorite sauce on the side.

Variation Tip: Add some additional ground black pepper to the filling.

Nutritional Information Per Serving: Calories 562 | Fat 18.4g | Sodium 388mg | Carbs 42.3g | Fiber 7g | Sugar 8.9g | Protein 52.3g

Sweet & Spicy Chicken Sandwich

Prep Time: 15 minutes | Cook Time: 5 minutes | Serves: 1

Ingredients:

⅛ cup of apple cider vinegar
1 hamburger buns
⅛ cup of jalapeno jelly

½ teaspoons of salt
2 chicken breasts
½ teaspoons of Tabasco sauce

Preparation:

1. Mix Tabasco sauce, jalapeno jelly, apple cider vinegar, and salt in a bowl. 2. Preheat your Hamilton Beach Breakfast Sandwich Maker. 3. Lift the top cover, ring, and cooking plate. 4. Place the lower half of a bun in the sandwich maker. 5. Now lower the cooking plate and top rings, then add chicken and the sauce. 6. Place the other top half of the bun on top. 7. Cover the top hood, and let the sandwich cook for 5 minutes. 8. When finished cooking, rotate the handle of the cooking plate clockwise until it stops. 9. Lift the hood, the rings and transfer the sandwich to a plate. 10. Serve.

Serving Suggestion: Serve the sandwich with crispy bacon and your favorite sauce on the side.

Variation Tip: You can add a lettuce leave to the filling as well.

Nutritional Information Per Serving: Calories 529| Fat 38g| Sodium 663mg | Carbs 4g | Fiber 1g | Sugar 8g | Protein 42g

Turkey and Mushroom Sandwich

Prep Time: 15 minutes | Cook Time: 5 minutes | Serves: 1

Ingredients:

2 teaspoons of grated Parmesan cheese
2 slices of turkey breast
2 tablespoons of cream of chicken soup
2 white bread slices, cut in 4-inch circle

1 teaspoon of light cream
2 slices of bacon
1 teaspoon of lemon juice
6 mushroom caps

Preparation:

1. Top with light cream, cream of chicken soup, mushrooms, lemon juice. 2. Preheat your Hamilton Beach Breakfast Sandwich Maker. 3. Lift the top cover, ring, and cooking plate. 4. Place one bread round in the sandwich maker. 5. Now lower the cooking plate and top rings, then add the fillings on top. 6. Add the other circle of the bread on top. 7. Cover the top hood, and let the sandwich cook for 5 minutes. 8. When finished cooking, rotate the handle of the cooking plate clockwise until it stops. 9. Lift the hood, the rings and transfer the sandwich to a plate. 10. Serve.

Serving Suggestion: Serve the sandwich with coleslaw and your favorite sauce on the side.
Variation Tip: Add some additional ground black pepper to the filling.
Nutritional Information Per Serving: Calories 381| Fat 26g |Sodium 970mg | Carbs 10g | Fiber 0g | Sugar 3.7g | Protein 26g

Spicy Curried Turkey Burgers

Prep time: 15 minutes | Cook Time: 15 minutes | Serves: 4

Ingredients:

½ lb. turkey mince
½ red onion, grated
1 garlic clove, crushed
2 teaspoons madras curry powder
1 handful chopped coriander

1 egg yolk
1 tablespoon sunflower oil
4 burger buns, split in half
4 tablespoons mango chutney

Preparation:

1. Blend turkey with red onion, garlic, curry powder, coriander, and egg yolk in a food processor for 1 minute. 2. Set a suitable skillet with olive oil over medium-high heat. 3. Make four equal-sized patties out of the turkey mixture. 4. Sear the turkey patties in the oil for 5 minutes per side. 5. Preheat your Hamilton Beach Breakfast Sandwich Maker until PREHEAT light gets green. 6. Lift the top cover, ring, and cooking plate. 7. Place half of a bun, cut-side up, inside the bottom tray of the sandwich maker. 8. Spread ¼ of the mango chutney on top. 9. Now lower the cooking plate and top rings then place a patty. 10. Place the other top half of the bun on top. 11. Cover the top hood, and let the sandwich cook for 5 minutes. 12. Rotate the handle of the cooking plate clockwise until it stops. 13. Lift the hood, the rings and transfer the sandwich to a plate. 14. Repeat the same steps with the remaining ingredients. 15. Serve.

Serving Suggestion: Serve the sandwich with a cauliflower bacon salad on the side.
Variation Tip: Enjoy sautéed veggies on the side for a change of taste.
Nutritional Information Per Serving: Calories 376 | Fat 17g |Sodium 1127mg | Carbs 34g | Fiber 1g | Sugar 3g | Protein 29g

Chicken and Red Cabbage Sandwich

Prep Time: 15 minutes | Cook Time: 5 minutes | Serves: 1

Ingredients:

1 French bun, split
1 cup of shredded red cabbage
1 small onion

1 boneless chicken breast, cooked and sliced
¼ cup of island salad dressing
½ cup of Swiss cheese

Preparation:

1. Preheat your Hamilton Beach Breakfast Sandwich Maker. 2. Lift the top cover, ring, and cooking plate. 3. Place one bread round in the sandwich maker. 4. Top it with chicken breast slices. 5. Now lower the cooking plate and top rings, then add the rest of the fillings on top. 6. Add the other circle of the bread on top. 7. Cover the top hood, and let the sandwich cook for 5 minutes. 8. When finished cooking, rotate the handle of the cooking plate clockwise until it stops. 9. Lift the hood, the rings and transfer the sandwich to a plate. 10. Serve.

Serving Suggestion: Serve the sandwich with your favorite sauce on the side.
Variation Tip: You can add a lettuce leave to the filling as well.
Nutritional Information Per Serving: Calories 525 | Fat 19g | Sodium 230mg | Carbs 17g | Fiber 3.8g | Sugar 8.5g | Protein 67g

Smoked Turkey and Cucumber Sandwich

Prep Time: 15 minutes | Cook Time: 5 minutes | Serves: 1

Ingredients:

2 pieces of pumpernickel bread, cut in 4-inch circle
1½ tablespoons of non-fat mayonnaise
1 small red onion
2 sprigs of fresh dill, chopped
2 slices of smoked turkey breast

1 teaspoon of capers
¼ teaspoons of ground black pepper
3 thin slices of cucumber
½ teaspoons of dried dill

Preparation:

1. In a small bowl, mix capers, mayonnaise, pepper, and dill. 2. Preheat the Breakfast Sandwich Maker until the green PREHEAT light comes on. Lift cover, top ring, and cooking plate. 3. Place one bread round in the bottom ring of the sandwich maker. 4. Lower the cooking plate and top ring. Add the turkey breasts and remaining fillings to the cooking plate. Spread the caper mix on top. 5. Then top with the other circle of the bread. 6. Close the cover and cook for 5 minutes. Rotate the cooking plate handle clockwise until it stops. Then lift the cover and rings and carefully remove the sandwich with plastic spatula. 7. Serve.

Serving Suggestion: Serve the sandwich with crispy bacon and your favorite sauce on the side.

Variation Tip: You can add a drizzle of paprika on top of the filling as well.

Nutritional Information Per Serving: Calories 356 | Fat 12.7g |Sodium 293mg | Carbs 7.9g | Fiber 0.3g | Sugar 7.9g | Protein 49.5g

Chicken, Green Chiles and Avocado Pita Sandwich

Prep Time: 15 minutes | Cook Time: 5 minutes | Serves: 1

Ingredients:

1 pita bread, split, cut in 4-inch circle
1 small onion
1 teaspoon of lemon juice
¼ teaspoons of salt
2 tablespoons of Monterey Jack cheese, shredded
1 teaspoon of vegetable oil

1 tablespoon of taco sauce
½ cup of cooked chicken
½ cup of shredded lettuce
1 ounce of green chilies
1 tablespoon of sour cream
1 small sliced avocado

Preparation:

1. Sprinkle salt and lemon juice on avocado. 2. Mix onion, salt, chilies, oil, taco sauce, and chicken together. 3. Top with the avocado mix, lettuce, and cheese. 4. Preheat your Hamilton Beach Breakfast Sandwich Maker. 5. Lift the top cover, ring, and cooking plate. 6. Place one bread round in the sandwich maker. 7. Now lower the cooking plate and top rings, then add the fillings on top. 8. Add the other circle of the bread on top. 9. Cover the top hood, and let the sandwich cook for 5 minutes. 10. When finished cooking, rotate the handle of the cooking plate clockwise until it stops. 11. Lift the hood, the rings and transfer the sandwich to a plate. 12. Serve.

Serving Suggestion: Serve the sandwich with your favorite sauce on the side.

Variation Tip: You can add a layer of your favorite sauce to the filling as well.

Nutritional Information Per Serving: Calories 529 | Fat 17g | Sodium 391mg | Carbs 55g | Fiber 6g | Sugar 8g | Protein 41g

Honey-Mustard Turkey Burgers

Prep time: 15 minutes | Cook Time: 15 minutes | Serves: 4

Ingredients:

¼ cup mustard
2 tablespoons honey
1 lb. ground turkey breast
¼ teaspoon salt
¼ teaspoon black pepper

2 teaspoons canola oil
4 whole-wheat hamburger buns, split
4 lettuce leaves
4 tomato slices
4 red onion slices

Preparation:

1. Blend turkey with salt, honey, mustard and black pepper in a food processor for 1 minute. 2. Set a suitable skillet with olive oil over medium-high heat. 3. Make 4 equal-sized patties out of the turkey mixture. 4. Sear the turkey patties in the oil for 5 minutes per side. 5. Preheat your Hamilton Beach Breakfast Sandwich Maker until PREHEAT light gets green. 6. Lift the top cover, ring, and cooking plate. 7. Place half of a bun, cut-side up, inside the bottom tray of the sandwich maker. 8. Now lower the cooking plate and top rings then place a patty, a lettuce leaf, 1 onion slice and tomato slice on top. 9. Place the other top half of the bun on top. 10. Cover the top hood, and let the sandwich cook for 5 minutes. 11. Rotate the handle of the cooking plate clockwise until it stops. 12. Lift the hood, the rings and transfer the sandwich to a plate. 13. Repeat the same steps with the remaining ingredients. 14. Serve.

Serving Suggestion: Serve the sandwich with crispy bacon and your favorite sauce on the side.
Variation Tip: Add a layer of pickled veggies for a change of taste.
Nutritional Information Per Serving: Calories 337 | Fat 20g |Sodium 719mg | Carbs 21g | Fiber 0.9g | Sugar 1.4g | Protein 37.8g

Chipotle Turkey-Avocado Sliders

Prep time: 15 minutes | Cook Time: 25 minutes | Serves: 3

Ingredients:

1 small red onion, sliced
½ cup white vinegar
½ cup water
2 teaspoons sugar
¾ teaspoon salt
1 lb. lean ground turkey
¼ cup chopped fresh cilantro

2 teaspoons ground cumin
6 teaspoons mayonnaise
¾ teaspoon ground chipotle pepper
2 roma tomatoes, cut into 6 slices each
6 ripe baby avocados, halved, pitted and peeled
3 leaves green-leaf lettuce, halved
½ teaspoon sesame seeds

Preparation:

1. Blend turkey with onion, white vinegar, sugar, salt, cilantro, cumin, chipotle pepper in a food processor for 1 minute. 2. Set a suitable skillet with olive oil over medium-high heat. 3. Make 3 equal-sized patties out of the turkey mixture. 4. Sear the turkey patties in the oil for 5 minutes per side then transfer them to a plate. 5. Mash avocado in a bowl, drop ⅙ of the mash into the skillet, spread it into a 4 inch round and cook for 2-3 minutes per side. 6. Make more pancakes in the same way. 7. Preheat your Hamilton Beach Breakfast Sandwich Maker until PREHEAT light gets green. 8. Lift the top cover, ring, and cooking plate. 9. Place an avocado cake inside the bottom tray of the sandwich maker then add 1 teaspoon mayo. 10. Now lower the cooking plate and top rings then place a patty, a lettuce leaf, and a tomato slice on top. 11. Place another avocado pancake on top. 12. Cover the top hood, and let the sandwich cook for 5 minutes. 13. Rotate the handle of the cooking plate clockwise until it stops. 14. Lift the hood, the rings and transfer the sandwich to a plate. Sprinkle with sesame seeds. 15. Repeat the same steps with the remaining ingredients. 16. Serve.

Serving Suggestion: Serve the sandwich with crispy sweet potato fries on the side.
Variation Tip: Add a layer of pickled onions for a change of taste.
Nutritional Information Per Serving: Calories 282 | Fat 15g |Sodium 526mg | Carbs 20g | Fiber 0.6g | Sugar 3.3g | Protein 16g

Herbed Chicken and Bacon Burgers

Prep time: 15 minutes | Cook Time: 50 minutes | Serves: 8

Ingredients:

Burgers
2 tablespoons olive oil
½ medium red onion, minced
4 garlic cloves, minced
2 lbs. ground chicken meat
½ teaspoon salt
To serve
8 burger buns, split in half
1 onion, sliced
8 lettuce leaves

1 teaspoon black pepper
½ cup chopped parsley
1 tablespoon fresh rosemary
1 tablespoon fresh sage
2 teaspoons fresh thyme, chopped

8 tomato slices
8 bacon slices, cooked

Preparation:

1. Blend chicken with red onion, garlic, salt, black pepper, parsley, rosemary, sage and thyme in a food processor for 1 minute. 2. Set a suitable skillet with olive oil over medium-high heat. 3. Make eight equal-sized patties out of the turkey mixture. 4. Sear the chicken patties in the oil for 5 minutes per side. 5. Preheat your Hamilton Beach Breakfast Sandwich Maker until PREHEAT light gets green. 6. Lift the top cover, ring, and cooking plate. 7. Place half of a bun, cut-side up, inside the bottom tray of the sandwich maker. 8. Now lower the cooking plate and top rings, then place a patty, an onion slice, a lettuce leaf and a tomato slice on top. 9. Place the other top half of the bun on top. 10. Cover the top hood, and let the sandwich cook for 5 minutes. 11. Rotate the handle of the cooking plate clockwise until it stops. 12. Lift the hood, the rings and transfer the sandwich to a plate. 13. Repeat the same steps with the remaining ingredients. 14. Serve.
Serving Suggestion: Serve the sandwich with a broccoli salad on the side.
Variation Tip: Add a layer of pickled onions for a change of taste.
Nutritional Information Per Serving: Calories 457 | Fat 19g |Sodium 557mg | Carbs 29g | Fiber 1.8g | Sugar 1.2g | Protein 32.5g

Herbed Turkey and Cranberry Burgers

Prep time: 15 minutes | Cook Time: 15 minutes | Serves: 4

Ingredients:

¼ cup (2 tablespoons) whole-wheat couscous
½ cup boiling water
2 tablespoons olive oil
1 small onion, chopped
1 stalk celery, minced
1 tablespoon fresh thyme, chopped

1 ½ teaspoon fresh sage, chopped
½ teaspoon salt
½ teaspoon black pepper
¼ cup dried cranberries, chopped
1 lb. 93%-lean ground turkey
4 buns, cut in half

Preparation:

1. Boil couscous with water until soft then drain. 2. Blend turkey with couscous, onion, celery, thyme, sage, salt, black pepper, and cranberries in a food processor for 1 minute. 3. Set a suitable skillet with olive oil over medium-high heat. 4. Make 4 equal-sized patties out of this mixture. 5. Sear the turkey patties in the oil for 5 minutes per side. 6. Preheat your Hamilton Beach Breakfast Sandwich Maker until PREHEAT light gets green. 7. Lift the top cover, ring, and cooking plate. 8. Place half of a bun, cut-side up, inside the bottom tray of the sandwich maker. 9. Now lower the cooking plate and top rings then place a patty on top. 10. Place the other top half of the bun on top. 11. Cover the top hood, and let the sandwich cook for 5 minutes. 12. Rotate the handle of the cooking plate clockwise until it stops. 13. Lift the hood, the rings and transfer the sandwich to a plate. 14. Repeat the same steps with the remaining ingredients. 15. Serve.
Serving Suggestion: Serve the sandwich with crispy fries on the side.
Variation Tip: you can add a lettuce leaf to the filling as well.
Nutritional Information Per Serving: Calories 273 | Fat 22g |Sodium 517mg | Carbs 3.3g | Fiber 0.2g | Sugar 1.4g | Protein 16.1g

Chili Turkey and Cilantro Burgers

Prep time: 15 minutes | Cook Time: 15 minutes | Serves: 2

Ingredients:

1 lb. ground turkey
3 tablespoons fresh cilantro, chopped
1 scallion, minced
2 teaspoons chili powder
1 teaspoon ground cumin
½ teaspoon sea salt

½ teaspoon black pepper
4 green chiles
4 slices pepper jack cheese
2-inch flour tortillas, cut into 4 inches rounds
4 tablespoons sour cream

Preparation:

1. Blend turkey with cilantro, scallion, chili powder, cumin, salt, and black pepper in a food processor for 1 minute. 2. Set a suitable skillet with olive oil over medium-high heat. 3. Make 4 equal-sized patties out of the turkey mixture. 4. Sear the turkey patties in the oil for 5 minutes per side. 5. Preheat your Hamilton Beach Breakfast Sandwich Maker until PREHEAT light gets green. 6. Lift the top cover, ring, and cooking plate. 7. Place a tortilla round inside the bottom tray of the sandwich maker. 8. Now lower the cooking plate and top rings then place a patty, green chile, a cheese slice and 1 tablespoon sour cream on top. 9. Place another tortilla round on top. 10. Cover the top hood, and let the sandwich cook for 5 minutes. 11. Rotate the handle of the cooking plate clockwise until it stops. 12. Lift the hood, the rings and transfer the sandwich to a plate. 13. Repeat the same steps with the remaining ingredients. 14. Serve.

Serving Suggestion: Serve the sandwich with crispy zucchini fries on the side.

Variation Tip: you can add a lettuce leaf to the filling as well.

Nutritional Information Per Serving: Calories 305 | Fat 25g |Sodium 532mg | Carbs 2.3g | Fiber 0.4g | Sugar 2g | Protein 18.3g

Cheese Turkey Mushroom Burgers

Prep time: 15 minutes | Cook Time: 15 minutes | Serves: 4

Ingredients:

2 tablespoons olive oil
1 garlic clove, minced
¾ teaspoon black pepper
½ teaspoon salt
8 Portobello mushroom caps
1 lb. lean ground turkey

2 teaspoons Worcestershire sauce
1 teaspoon Dijon mustard
4 slices Swiss cheese
1 small tomato, sliced
3 cups baby arugula

Preparation:

1. Blend turkey with garlic, black pepper, salt, and Worcestershire sauce in a food processor for 1 minute. 2. Set a suitable skillet with olive oil over medium-high heat. 3. Make 4 equal-sized patties out of the turkey mixture. 4. Sear the turkey patties in the oil for 5 minutes per side. 5. Preheat your Hamilton Beach Breakfast Sandwich Maker until PREHEAT light gets green. 6. Lift the top cover, ring, and cooking plate. 7. Place a Portobello mushroom cap, cut-side up, inside the bottom tray of the sandwich maker. 8. Now lower the cooking plate and top rings then place a patty, ¼ Swiss cheese, tomato, and arugula on top. 9. Place the other mushroom cap on top. 10. Cover the top hood, and let the sandwich cook for 5 minutes. 11. Rotate the handle of the cooking plate clockwise until it stops. 12. Lift the hood, the rings and transfer the sandwich to a plate. 13. Repeat the same steps with the remaining ingredients. 14. Serve.

Serving Suggestion: Serve the sandwich with crispy sweet potato fries on the side.

Variation Tip: you can add a lettuce leaf to the filling as well.

Nutritional Information Per Serving: Calories 321 | Fat 7.4g |Sodium 356mg | Carbs 29.3g | Fiber 2.4g | Sugar 5g | Protein 37.2g

Chapter 6 Vegetarian Breakfast Recipes

59 Cheese-Egg Biscuit

59 Raspberry Brie Pancake Sandwich

59 Ham and Salami Cheese Sandwich

60 Egg Whites Cheese Ciabatta Sandwich

60 Provolone Mushroom Cheese Sandwich

60 Egg and Cheese Bagel

61 Basil Tomato Cheese Sandwiches

61 Garlicky Tofu-Onion Burgers

62 Flavorful Spinach Sandwich

62 Cheese Apple Cinnamon Raisin Sandwich

62 Broccoli and Cucumber Sandwich

63 Mushroom, Avocado and Red Pepper Burgers

63 Cumin Black Bean Burgers

64 Black Bean and Brown Rice Beet Burgers

64 Red Cabbage and Jackfruit Burger

65 Garlic Chickpeas Burgers

65 Black Bean Potato Burgers

65 Avocado and Egg Cheese Sandwich

66 Black Bean and Tomato Burgers

66 Tempeh Carrot Tomato Sandwich

Cheese-Egg Biscuit

Prep Time: 15 minutes | Cook Time: 5 minutes | Serves: 1

Ingredients:

1 biscuit, sliced
1 slice cheddar cheese
1 slice red onion

1 slice green pepper, seeded and cored
1 large egg, beaten

Preparation:

1. Preheat the Breakfast Sandwich Maker until the green PREHEAT light comes on. Lift cover, top ring, and cooking plate. 2. Place half of biscuit in bottom ring of Breakfast Sandwich Maker. Top the biscuit with a slice of cheddar cheese along with the red onion and green pepper. 3. Lower cooking plate and top ring. Crack the egg into the cooking plate. 4. Top the egg with the other top half of the biscuit. 5. Close the cover and cook for 5 minutes. Rotate the cooking plate handle clockwise until it stops. Then lift the cover and rings and carefully remove the sandwich with plastic spatula. 6. Serve.

Serving Suggestion: Serve the sandwich with your favorite sauce on the side.

Variation Tip: Add some additional dried herbs to the filling.

Nutritional Information Per Serving: Calories 496 | Fat 20.5g | Sodium 1885mg | Carbs 6.5g | Fiber 0.3g | Sugar 5.2g | Protein 67.7g

Raspberry Brie Pancake Sandwich

Prep Time: 15 minutes | Cook Time: 5 minutes | Serves: 1

Ingredients:

2 frozen pancakes
1 tablespoon raspberry jam

1-ounce Brie, chopped
1 large egg

Preparation:

1. Preheat the Breakfast Sandwich Maker until the green PREHEAT light comes on. Lift cover, top ring, and cooking plate. 2. Place one pancake in bottom ring of Breakfast Sandwich Maker. 3. Lower cooking plate and top ring. Crack the egg into the cooking plate. Spread the jam and chopped brie. Top with another pancake. 4. Close the cover and cook for 5 minutes. Rotate the cooking plate handle clockwise until it stops. Then lift the cover and rings and carefully remove the sandwich with plastic spatula. 5. Serve.

Serving Suggestion: Serve the sandwich with crispy bacon and your favorite sauce on the side.

Variation Tip: You can add a drizzle of lemon juice on top of the filling as well.

Nutritional Information Per Serving: Calories 315 | Fat 20.1g | Sodium 67mg | Carbs 1.9g | Fiber 0.2g | Sugar 0.7g | Protein 30.4g

Ham and Salami Cheese Sandwich

Prep Time: 15 minutes | Cook Time: 5 minutes | Serves: 1

Ingredients:

2 slices thick white bread, cut in 4-inch circle
1 slice deli ham
1 slice hard salami
1 slice provolone cheese
1 tablespoon chopped black olives

1 tablespoon roasted red pepper, chopped
1 teaspoon minced red onion
1 garlic clove, minced
Salt and black pepper to taste
1 large egg

Preparation:

1. In a small bowl, mix together the olives, red onion, red pepper and garlic. Season with salt and pepper and stir well. 2. Preheat the Breakfast Sandwich Maker until the green PREHEAT light comes on. Lift cover, top ring, and cooking plate. 3. Place one of the bread slices in the bottom ring of the sandwich maker. 4. Top the bread with ham and salami. Then spread the olive mixture. Then add one slice of provolone cheese on top. 5. Lower cooking plate and top ring. Crack the egg into the cooking plate. 6. Top with the other circle of the bread. 7. Close the cover and cook for 5 minutes. Rotate the cooking plate handle clockwise until it stops. Then lift the cover and rings and carefully remove the sandwich with plastic spatula. 8. Serve.

Serving Suggestion: Serve the sandwich with crispy bacon and your favorite sauce on the side.

Variation Tip: You can add a layer of your favorite sauce to the filling as well.

Nutritional Information Per Serving: Calories 361 | Fat 16g |Sodium 515mg | Carbs 19.3g | Fiber 0.1g | Sugar 18.2g | Protein 33.3g

Egg Whites Cheese Ciabatta Sandwich

Prep Time: 15 minutes | Cook Time: 5 minutes | Serves: 1

Ingredients:

1 ciabatta sandwich bun, sliced
1 teaspoon unsalted butter
1 slice mozzarella cheese
2 large egg whites

1 tablespoon skim milk
1 garlic clove, minced
1 teaspoon chopped chives
⅛ teaspoon dried Italian seasoning

Preparation:

1. Preheat the Breakfast Sandwich Maker until the green PREHEAT light comes on. Lift cover, top ring, and cooking plate. 2. Place half of the bun, cut-side up, in the bottom ring of the sandwich maker. 3. Spread the butter over the ciabatta bun. Add one slice of mozzarella cheese on top. 4. In a small bowl, whisk together the egg whites, milk, chives, garlic and Italian seasoning. 5. Lower cooking plate and top ring. Pour in the egg mixture. 6. Top with the other top half of the bun. 7. Close the cover and cook for 5 minutes. Rotate the cooking plate handle clockwise until it stops. Then lift the cover and rings and carefully remove the sandwich with plastic spatula. 8. Serve.

Serving Suggestion: Serve the sandwich with coleslaw and your favorite sauce on the side.

Variation Tip: Add some additional ground black pepper to the filling.

Nutritional Information Per Serving: Calories 545 | Fat 36g | Sodium 272mg | Carbs 41g | Fiber 0.2g | Sugar 0.1g | Protein 42.5g

Provolone Mushroom Cheese Sandwich

Prep Time: 15 minutes | Cook Time: 5 minutes | Serves: 1

Ingredients:

1 whole wheat English muffin, sliced
1 teaspoon olive oil
1 portabella mushroom cap

1 slice provolone cheese
1 large egg, beaten
½ cup spring greens

Preparation:

1. Preheat the Breakfast Sandwich Maker until the green PREHEAT light comes on. Lift cover, top ring, and cooking plate. 2. Place half of the muffin, cut-side up, in bottom ring of the sandwich maker. 3. Brush the muffin with olive oil. 4. Top with the mushroom cap and one slice of provolone cheese. 5. Lower cooking plate and top ring. Pour in the beaten egg. 6. Add the greens and top with another muffin half. 7. Close the cover and cook for 5 minutes. Rotate the cooking plate handle clockwise until it stops. Then lift the cover and rings and carefully remove the sandwich with plastic spatula. 8. Serve.

Serving Suggestion: Serve the sandwich with crispy bacon and your favorite sauce on the side.

Variation Tip: Add some additional dried herbs to the filling.

Nutritional Information Per Serving: Calories 448 | Fat 19.3g | Sodium 261mg | Carbs 0.5g | Fiber 0.3g | Sugar 0.1g | Protein 64.1g

Egg and Cheese Bagel

Prep Time: 15 minutes | Cook Time: 5 minutes | Serves: 1

Ingredients:

1 poppy seed bagel, sliced
1-ounce goat cheese
1 large egg

1 teaspoon chopped chives
Salt and black pepper to taste

Preparation:

1. Preheat the Breakfast Sandwich Maker until the green PREHEAT light comes on. Lift cover, top ring, and cooking plate. 2. Place half of the bagel, cut-side up, in bottom ring of the sandwich maker. 3. Spread the goat cheese over the bagel. 4. In a small bowl, whisk the egg with chopped chives, salt and pepper. 5. Lower the cooking plate and top ring, then pour in the egg mixture. 6. Top with the other half of the bagel. 7. Close the cover and cook for 5 minutes. Rotate the cooking plate handle clockwise until it stops. Then lift the cover and rings and carefully remove the sandwich with plastic spatula. 8. Serve.

Serving Suggestion: Serve the sandwich with your favorite sauce on the side.

Variation Tip: You can add a lettuce leave to the filling as well.

Nutritional Information Per Serving: Calories 354; Fat 7.9g; Sodium 704mg; Carbs 6g; Fiber 3.6g; Sugar 6g; Protein 18g

Basil Tomato Cheese Sandwiches

Prep Time: 15 minutes | Cook Time: 10 minutes | Serves: 2

Ingredients:

1 round flatbread, cut in 4-inch circle
1 teaspoon olive oil
1 garlic clove, minced
1 slice mozzarella cheese
2 thin slices ripe tomato

1 thin slice red onion
4 fresh basil leaves
Pinch dried oregano
1 large egg, beaten
2 teaspoons grated parmesan cheese

Preparation:

1. Preheat the Breakfast Sandwich Maker until the green PREHEAT light comes on. Lift cover, top ring, and cooking plate. 2. Place half of the muffin, cut-side up, in bottom ring of the sandwich maker. 3. Brush the top with olive oil and sprinkle with garlic. 4. Add ½ of the tomatoes, red onion and basil leaves on top and sprinkle with dried oregano. 5. Then top the vegetables with ½ of the mozzarella cheese. 6. Lower cooking plate and top ring. Pour the beaten egg into the cooking plate. 7. Top with the other circle of the bread. 8. Close the cover and cook for 5 minutes. Rotate the cooking plate handle clockwise until it stops. Then lift the cover and rings and carefully remove the sandwich with plastic spatula. 9. Sprinkle the sandwich with parmesan cheese then enjoy. 10. Repeat the process for the remaining ingredients. 11. Serve.

Serving Suggestion: Serve the sandwich with your favorite sauce on the side.

Variation Tip: You can add a drizzle of paprika on top of the filling as well.

Nutritional Information Per Serving: Calories 336 | Fat 12.8g | Sodium 40mg | Carbs 4.2g | Fiber 1g | Sugar 0.7g | Protein 50.7g

Garlicky Tofu-Onion Burgers

Prep time: 15 minutes | Cook Time: 40 minutes | Serves: 6

Ingredients:

Burgers
½ (14-ounces) extra-firm tofu, drained
1 medium onion, diced
3 green onions, diced
2 tablespoons wheat germ
2 tablespoons all-purpose flour
Serving
6 hamburger buns
6 lettuce leaves

2 tablespoons garlic powder
2 tablespoons soy sauce
Dash of pepper
1 tablespoon oil for frying

6 slices tomato

Preparation:

1. Blend tofu with onion, green onions, wheat germ, flour, garlic powder, soy sauce, and black pepper in a food processor for 1 minute. 2. Set a suitable skillet with olive oil over medium-high heat. 3. Make 6 equal-sized patties out of the turkey mixture. 4. Sear the tofu patties in the oil for 5 minutes per side. 5. Preheat your Hamilton Beach Breakfast Sandwich Maker until PREHEAT light gets green. 6. Lift the top cover, ring, and cooking plate. 7. Place half of a bun, cut-side up, inside the bottom tray of the sandwich maker. 8. Now lower the cooking plate and top rings then place a patty, a lettuce leaf, and a tomato slice on top. 9. Place the other top half of the bun on top. 10. Cover the top hood, and let the burger cook for 5 minutes. 11. Rotate the handle of the cooking plate clockwise until it stops. 12. Lift the hood, the rings and transfer the burger to a plate. 13. Repeat the same steps with the remaining ingredients. 14. Serve.

Serving Suggestion: Serve the sandwich with crispy fries on the side.

Variation Tip: Add a layer of pickled veggies for a change of taste.

Nutritional Information Per Serving: Calories 180 | Fat 3.2g |Sodium 133mg | Carbs 32g | Fiber 1.1g | Sugar 1.8g | Protein 9g

Flavorful Spinach Sandwich

Prep Time: 15 minutes | Cook Time: 7 minutes | Serves: 1

Ingredients:

2 slices multigrain bread, cut in 4-inch circle
1 large egg, beaten
2 tablespoons plain nonfat yogurt
¼ teaspoon Dijon mustard

½ cup baby spinach
1 tablespoon minced yellow onion
1 teaspoon olive oil

Preparation:

1. Heat the oil in a suitable skillet over medium heat. Add the onion and spinach and stir well. 2. Cook for almost 2 minutes, stirring, until the spinach is just wilted. Set aside. 3. Preheat your Hamilton Beach Breakfast Sandwich Maker. 4. Lift the top cover, ring, and cooking plate. 5. Place one bread slice in the sandwich maker. 6. Whisk together the yogurt and mustard in a small bowl, then brush over the piece of bread. 7. Top the bread with the cooked spinach and onion mixture. 8. Now lower the cooking plate and top rings, then pour in the egg. 9. Add the other circle of the bread on top. 10. Cover the top hood, and let the sandwich cook for 5 minutes. 11. When finished cooking, rotate the handle of the cooking plate clockwise until it stops. 12. Lift the hood, the rings and transfer the sandwich to a plate. 13. Serve.

Serving Suggestion: Serve the sandwich with coleslaw and your favorite sauce on the side.

Variation Tip: Add some additional dried herbs to the filling.

Nutritional Information Per Serving: Calories 305 | Fat 12.7g |Sodium 227mg | Carbs 26.1g | Fiber 1.4g | Sugar 0.9g | Protein 35.2g

Cheese Apple Cinnamon Raisin Sandwich

Prep Time: 15 minutes | Cook Time: 5 minutes | Serves: 1

Ingredients:

2 slices cinnamon raisin bread, cut in 4-inch circle
½ small apple, sliced thin
1 thin slice cheddar cheese

½ teaspoon unsalted butter
Pinch ground cinnamon and nutmeg

Preparation:

1. Preheat your Hamilton Beach Breakfast Sandwich Maker. 2. Lift the top cover, ring, and cooking plate. 3. Place the lower half of the muffin in the sandwich maker. 4. Place one slice of bread inside the bottom tray of the sandwich maker. 5. Spread the bread with butter. 6. Now lower the cooking plate and top rings. 7. Top with the slices of apple, then sprinkle them with cinnamon and nutmeg. 8. Place the slice of cheddar cheese over the apples. 9. Top the cheese with the other piece of bread. 10. Cover the top hood, and let the sandwich cook for 5 minutes. 11. When finished cooking, rotate the handle of the cooking plate clockwise until it stops. 12. Lift the hood, the rings and transfer the sandwich to a plate. 13. Serve.

Serving Suggestion: Serve the sandwich with your favorite sauce on the side.

Variation Tip: Add some additional ground black pepper to the filling.

Nutritional Information Per Serving: Calories 432 | Fat 9.5g |Sodium 515.8mg | Carbs 33.2g | Fiber 0.2g | Sugar 0.1g | Protein 9.4g

Broccoli and Cucumber Sandwich

Prep time: 15 minutes | Cook Time: 5 minutes | Serves: 2

Ingredients:

4 slices thin-sliced bread, cut into 4 inches' rounds
½ avocado, peeled and sliced
⅛ teaspoon kosher salt
2 tablespoons plain hummus

8 slices tomato
8 slices cucumber
½ cup broccoli sprouts

Preparation:

1. Preheat your Hamilton Beach Breakfast Sandwich Maker until PREHEAT light gets green. 2. Lift the top cover, ring, and cooking plate. 3. Place a bread slice inside the bottom tray of the sandwich maker. 4. Spread ½ of the hummus, salt, avocado, tomato, cucumber, broccoli and another bread slice on top. 5. Now lower the cooking plate and top rings. 6. Place another bread slice on top. 7. Cover the top hood, and let the sandwich cook for 5 minutes. 8. Rotate the handle of the cooking plate clockwise until it stops. 9. Lift the hood, the rings and transfer the sandwich to a plate. 10. Repeat the same steps with the remaining ingredients. 11. Serve.

Serving Suggestion: Serve the sandwich with a broccoli salad on the side.

Variation Tip: Add a layer of sliced bell peppers for a change of taste.

Nutritional Information Per Serving: Calories 113 | Fat 3g |Sodium 152mg | Carbs 20g | Fiber 3g | Sugar 1.1g | Protein 3.5g

Mushroom, Avocado and Red Pepper Burgers

Prep time: 15 minutes | Cook Time: 30 minutes | Serves: 4

Ingredients:

4 Portobello mushrooms, cut in half horizontally
1 medium onion, cut into slices
3 tablespoons olive oil
¾ teaspoon salt
½ teaspoon black pepper

1 avocado, peeled and sliced
2 tablespoons yogurt
½ teaspoon garlic, minced
4 hamburger buns, split in half
4 jarred roasted red peppers

Preparation:

1. Blend mushroom, onion, salt, black pepper, avocado, yoghurt, and garlic in a food processor for 1 minute. 2. Set a suitable skillet with olive oil over medium-high heat. 3. Make 4 equal-sized patties out of the mushroom mixture. 4. Sear the mushroom patties in the oil for 5 minutes per side. 5. Preheat your Hamilton Beach Breakfast Sandwich Maker until PREHEAT light gets green. 6. Lift the top cover, ring, and cooking plate. 7. Place half of a bun, cut-side up, inside the bottom tray of the sandwich maker. 8. Now lower the cooking plate and top rings then place a patty and red pepper on top. 9. Place the other top half of the bun on top. 10. Cover the top hood, and let the burger cook for 5 minutes. 11. Rotate the handle of the cooking plate clockwise until it stops. 12. Lift the hood, the rings and transfer the burger to a plate. 13. Repeat the same steps with the remaining ingredients. 14. Serve.

Serving Suggestion: Serve the sandwich with crispy carrot chips on the side.
Variation Tip: you can add a lettuce leaf to the filling as well.
Nutritional Information Per Serving: Calories 282 | Fat 15g |Sodium 526mg | Carbs 20g | Fiber 0.6g | Sugar 3.3g | Protein 16g

Cumin Black Bean Burgers

Prep time: 15 minutes | Cook Time: 50 minutes | Serves: 8

Ingredients:

2 (15-ounce) cans of black beans, drained
½ cup whole wheat flour
¼ cup yellow cornmeal
½ cup salsa

2 teaspoons ground cumin
1 teaspoon garlic salt
8 hamburger buns, split in half

Preparation:

1. Blend beans with whole wheat flour, cornmeal, salsa, cumin and salt in a food processor for 1 minute. 2. Set a suitable skillet with olive oil over medium-high heat. 3. Make 8 equal-sized patties out of the bean mixture. 4. Sear the bean patties in the oil for 5 minutes per side. 5. Preheat your Hamilton Beach Breakfast Sandwich Maker until PREHEAT light gets green. 6. Lift the top cover, ring, and cooking plate. 7. Place half of a bun, cut-side up, inside the bottom tray of the sandwich maker. 8. Now lower the cooking plate and top rings, then place a patty on top. 9. Place the other top half of the bun on top. 10. Cover the top hood, and let the burger cook for 5 minutes. 11. Rotate the handle of the cooking plate clockwise until it stops. 12. Lift the hood, the rings and transfer the burger to a plate. 13. Repeat the same steps with the remaining ingredients. 14. Serve.

Serving Suggestion: Serve the sandwich with crispy sweet potato fries on the side.
Variation Tip: Add a layer of spicy mayo and pickled veggies for a change of taste.
Nutritional Information Per Serving: Calories 209 | Fat 7.5g |Sodium 321mg | Carbs 34.1g | Fiber 4g | Sugar 3.8g | Protein 4.3g

Black Bean and Brown Rice Beet Burgers

Prep time: 15 minutes | Cook Time: 30 minutes | Serves: 4

Ingredients:

¼ cup uncooked brown rice
¾ cup water
1 shallot, peeled and quartered
1 large beet, peeled and quartered
1 cup canned black beans, rinsed and drained
1 large egg
½ cup breadcrumbs

2 tablespoons fresh parsley, chopped
1 teaspoon ground cumin
¼ teaspoon black pepper
¼ teaspoon kosher salt
4 seeded buns, split
1 cup baby arugula
Tahini, or Tzatziki, for serving

Preparation:

1. Cook rice with ¾ cup water in a saucepan until soft, then drain. 2. Boil beet in a pot filled with water until soft then peel and chop. 3. Blend black beans with rice, beet, egg, crumbs, parsley, cumin, black pepper, and salt in a food processor for 1 minute. 4. Set a suitable skillet with olive oil over medium-high heat. 5. Make 4 equal-sized patties out of the black bean mixture. 6. Sear the bean patties in the oil for 5 minutes per side. 7. Preheat your Hamilton Beach Breakfast Sandwich Maker until PREHEAT light gets green. 8. Lift the top cover, ring, and cooking plate. 9. Place half of a bun, cut-side up, inside the bottom tray of the sandwich maker. 10. Now lower the cooking plate and top rings, then place a bean patty and ¼ cup arugula on top. 11. Place the other top half of the bun on top. 12. Cover the top hood, and let the burger cook for 5 minutes. 13. Rotate the handle of the cooking plate clockwise until it stops. 14. Lift the hood, the rings and transfer the burger to a plate. 15. Repeat the same steps with the remaining ingredients. 16. Serve

Serving Suggestion: Serve the sandwich with a broccoli salad on the side.

Variation Tip: Enjoy sautéed veggies on the side for a change of taste.

Nutritional Information Per Serving: Calories 199 | Fat 11.1g |Sodium 297mg | Carbs 14.9g | Fiber 1g | Sugar 2.5g | Protein 9.9g

Red Cabbage and Jackfruit Burger

Prep time: 15 minutes | Cook Time: 30 minutes | Serves: 2

Ingredients:

½ lb. tin jackfruit
5 tablespoons jerk barbecue marinade
¼ red cabbage, shredded
1 carrot, peeled and ribboned
2 spring onions, chopped

5 tablespoons vegan mayonnaise
2 vegan burger buns, cut in half
1 tablespoon chopped fresh coriander
Salt and black pepper, to taste

Preparation:

1. Mix jackfruits with jerk barbecue marinade, peeled carrot, coriander, black pepper, salt, cabbage, carrot, spring onions on a baking sheet. 2. At 350 degrees F, preheat your oven. 3. Bake the jackfruit mixture for 20 minutes then shred it with a fork. 4. Preheat your Hamilton Beach Breakfast Sandwich Maker until PREHEAT light gets green. 5. Lift the top cover, ring, and cooking plate. 6. Place half of a bun, cut-side up, inside the bottom tray of the sandwich maker. 7. Add ½ of the mayonnaise, and jackfruit. 8. Now lower the cooking plate and top rings. 9. Place the other top half of the muffin on top. 10. Cover the top hood, and let the burger cook for 5 minutes. 11. Rotate the handle of the cooking plate clockwise until it stops. 12. Lift the hood, the rings and transfer the burger to a plate. 13. Repeat the same steps with the remaining ingredients. 14. Serve.

Serving Suggestion: Serve the sandwich with a cauliflower bacon salad on the side.

Variation Tip: you can add a lettuce leaf to the filling as well.

Nutritional Information Per Serving: Calories 282 | Fat 15g |Sodium 526mg | Carbs 20g | Fiber 0.6g | Sugar 3.3g | Protein 16g

Garlic Chickpeas Burgers

Prep time: 15 minutes | Cook Time: 27 minutes | Serves: 4

Ingredients:

1 teaspoon canola oil
¼ cup chopped onion
1 garlic clove minced
1½ cups canned chickpeas, drained

3 tablespoons frank's red hot sauce
1 tablespoon non-dairy butter
¼ teaspoon granulated onion
4 hamburger buns, split in half

Preparation:

1. Sauté chickpeas with oil, onion, garlic, red hot sauce, onion and butter in a skillet for 7 minutes. 2. Preheat your Hamilton Beach Breakfast Sandwich Maker until PREHEAT light gets green. 3. Lift the top cover, ring, and cooking plate. 4. Place half of a bun, cut-side up, inside the bottom tray of the sandwich maker. 5. Spread ¼ of the chickpeas over the bun. 6. Now lower the cooking plate and top rings. 7. Place the other top half of the muffin on top. 8. Cover the top hood, and let the burger cook for 5 minutes. 9. Rotate the handle of the cooking plate clockwise until it stops. 10. Lift the hood, the rings and transfer the burger to a plate. 11. Repeat the same steps with the remaining ingredients. 12. Serve.

Serving Suggestion: Serve the sandwich with crispy fries on the side.

Variation Tip: Add a layer of spicy mayo and pickled veggies for a change of taste.

Nutritional Information Per Serving: Calories 282 | Fat 15g |Sodium 526mg | Carbs 20g | Fiber 0.6g | Sugar 3.3g | Protein 16g

Black Bean Potato Burgers

Prep time: 15 minutes | Cook Time: 25 minutes | Serves: 3

Ingredients:

1 (15-ounce) can black beans, drained
1 medium carrot, grated
½ medium onion, chopped
3 medium potatoes, half-boiled, peeled and grated

4 large scallions, chopped
1 cup corn, fresh
½ teaspoon garlic salt
2 tablespoons olive oil

Preparation:

1. Blend black beans with onion, scallions, corn, salt, and carrot in a food processor for 1 minute. 2. Make 3 equal-sized patties out of the black bean mixture. 3. Set a suitable skillet with olive oil over medium-high heat. 4. Sear the bean patties in the oil for 5 minutes per side. 5. Preheat your Hamilton Beach Breakfast Sandwich Maker until PREHEAT light gets green. 6. Lift the top cover, ring, and cooking plate. 7. Add ⅙ of the grated potato, inside the bottom tray of the sandwich maker. 8. Now lower the cooking plate and top rings then place a bean patty on top. 9. Place ⅙ of the grated potatoes on top and drizzle oil on top. 10. Cover the top hood, and let the burger cook for 5 minutes. 11. Rotate the handle of the cooking plate clockwise until it stops. 12. Lift the hood, the rings and transfer the burger to a plate. 13. Repeat the same steps with the remaining ingredients. 14. Serve.

Serving Suggestion: Serve the sandwich with a cauliflower bacon salad on the side.

Variation Tip: Add a layer of sliced bell peppers for a change of taste.

Nutritional Information Per Serving: Calories 237 | Fat 19g |Sodium 518mg | Carbs 7g | Fiber 1.5g | Sugar 3.4g | Protein 12g

Avocado and Egg Cheese Sandwich

Prep Time: 15 minutes | Cook Time: 5 minutes | Serves: 1

Ingredients:

1 croissant, sliced
2 slices ripe tomato
¼ ripe avocado, pitted and sliced
1 slice Swiss cheese

1 large egg
1 tablespoon sliced green onion
2 teaspoons half-n-half

Preparation:

1. In a small bowl, whisk together the egg, green onion and half-n-half. 2. Preheat the Breakfast Sandwich Maker until the green PREHEAT light comes on. Lift cover, top ring, and cooking plate. 3. Place half of the croissant, cut-side up, in bottom ring of the sandwich maker. 4. Add the tomato, avocado, and a slice of Swiss cheese on top. 5. Lower cooking plate and top ring. Pour in the egg mixture. 6. Top with the other top half of the croissant. 7. Close the cover and cook for 5 minutes. Rotate the cooking plate handle clockwise until it stops. Then lift the cover and rings and carefully remove the sandwich with plastic spatula. 8. Serve.

Serving Suggestion: Serve the sandwich with your favorite sauce on the side.

Variation Tip: You can add a lettuce leave to the filling as well.

Nutritional Information Per Serving: Calories 548| Fat 22 g | Sodium 319 mg | Carbs 17 g | Fiber 3 g | Sugar 7.6 g | Protein 40 g

Black Bean and Tomato Burgers

Prep time: 15 minutes | Cook Time: 30 minutes | Serves: 4

Ingredients:

1 (14-ounce) can black beans, well-drained
2 tablespoons olive oil
2 slices bread, crumbled
½ medium onion, chopped
½ teaspoon seasoned salt
1 teaspoon garlic powder
1 teaspoon onion powder

1 dash black pepper
1 dash kosher salt
½ cup all-purpose flour
½ medium red onion, sliced
2 medium red heirloom tomatoes, sliced
6 leaves butter lettuce
4 buns, split

Preparation:

1. Blend black beans, crumbled bread, onion, salt, garlic powder, onion powder in a food processor for 1 minute. 2. Set a suitable skillet with olive oil over medium-high heat. 3. Make 4 equal-sized patties out of this bean mixture. 4. Sear the bean patties in the oil for 5 minutes per side. 5. Preheat your Hamilton Beach Breakfast Sandwich Maker until PREHEAT light gets green. 6. Lift the top cover, ring, and cooking plate. 7. Place half of a bun, cut-side up, inside the bottom tray of the sandwich maker. 8. Now lower the cooking plate and top rings, then place a patty, a lettuce leaf, an onion slice and a tomato slice on top. 9. Place the other top half of the bun on top. 10. Cover the top hood, and let the burger cook for 5 minutes. 11. Rotate the handle of the cooking plate clockwise until it stops. 12. Lift the hood, the rings and transfer the burger to a plate. 13. Repeat the same steps with the remaining ingredients. 14. Serve.
Serving Suggestion: Serve the sandwich with crispy zucchini fries on the side.
Variation Tip: Add a layer of pickled onions for a change of taste.
Nutritional Information Per Serving: Calories 229 | Fat 1.9 |Sodium 567mg | Carbs 1.9g | Fiber 0.4g | Sugar 0.6g | Protein 11.8g

Tempeh Carrot Tomato Sandwich

Prep time: 15 minutes | Cook Time: 15 minutes | Serves: 2

Ingredients:

2 large carrots, washed and peeled
1 (8 ounce) package tempeh, sliced
4 slices bread, cut into 4 inches' round
Marinade
¼ cup tamari
3 tablespoons maple syrup
¼ teaspoon onion powder
1 teaspoon liquid smoke

4 tablespoons vegan mayo
4 leaves romaine lettuce
2 large beefsteak tomatoes, sliced

2 teaspoons apple cider vinegar
¼ teaspoon smoked paprika
Black pepper, to taste

Preparation:

1. Mix all the marinade ingredients in a bowl and add tempeh. 2. Coat it well, cover and marinate for 30 minutes. 3. Sear the tempeh in a skillet with oil for 5 minutes per side. 4. Preheat your Hamilton Beach Breakfast Sandwich Maker until PREHEAT light gets green. 5. Lift the top cover, ring, and cooking plate. 6. Place a bread slice inside the bottom tray of the sandwich maker. 7. Add half of the mayo, tempeh, carrots, tomato and lettuce. 8. Place another bread slice on top. 9. Now lower the cooking plate and top rings. 10. Cover the top hood, and let the sandwich cook for 5 minutes. 11. Rotate the handle of the cooking plate clockwise until it stops. 12. Lift the hood, the rings and transfer the sandwich to a plate. 13. Repeat the same steps with the remaining ingredients. 14. Serve.
Serving Suggestion: Serve the sandwich with crispy bacon and your favorite sauce on the side.
Variation Tip: Add a layer of pickled veggies for a change of taste.
Nutritional Information Per Serving: Calories 284 | Fat 7.9g |Sodium 704mg | Carbs 38.1g | Fiber 1.9g | Sugar 1.9g | Protein 14.8g

Chapter 7 Fruit Breakfast Sandwich Recipes

68 Blueberry and Pear Croissant
68 Apple Sandwich
68 Honey Nuts Sandwich
69 Mango-Peach Sandwiches
69 Cheddar Apple Bacon Croissant
69 Apricot and Brie Croissant
70 Honey Pistachio Sandwich
70 Dark Chocolate-Avocado Sandwich
70 White Chocolate-Nut Sandwich
71 Mixed Fruit Sandwich
71 Japanese Strawberry & Kiwi Sandwich
71 Pumpkin-Apple Sandwich
72 Apple Raisin Sandwich

72 Ricotta Cheese Nectarine Biscuit
72 Bacon-Avocado Cheese Sandwich
73 Nutella-Avocado Cheese Sandwich
73 Nutella Raspberry Cheese Sandwich
73 Apple Nutella Sandwich
74 Delicious Peach Bran Sandwich
74 Chocolate-Hazelnut Banana Sandwich
74 Nutella Blueberry Sandwich
75 Dark Chocolate Cherry Sandwich
75 Homemade Peanut Butter Banana Sandwich
75 Strawberry Nutella Sandwich
76 Cinnamon Apple Sandwich

Blueberry and Pear Croissant

Prep Time: 15 minutes | Cook Time: 10 minutes | Serves: 2

Ingredients:

2 medium croissants, sliced in half

1 large pear (bosc pears are a perfect choice), sliced

2 tablespoons of honey

½ cup of blueberries, rinsed, drained and dried

3 tablespoons of cream cheese, brought to room temperature

Preparation:

1. Preheat the Breakfast Sandwich Maker until the green PREHEAT light comes on. Lift cover, top ring, and cooking plate. 2. Take 1½ teaspoons of the cream cheese and spread half on top of the croissant and half on the croissant bottom. 3. Place the croissant bottom in the bottom ring of the sandwich maker and top with half of the pear slices. 4. Add ¼ cup of blueberries on top of the pear slices. 5. Take a tablespoon of the honey and drizzle it over the fruit. 6. Lower cooking plate and top ring. Add egg to cooking plate. Then top with the other top half of croissant. 7. Close the cover and cook for 5 minutes. Rotate the cooking plate handle clockwise until it stops. Then lift the cover and rings and carefully remove the sandwich with plastic spatula. 8. Repeat the same steps with the remaining ingredients. 9. Serve.

Serving Suggestion: Serve the sandwich with crispy bacon and your favorite sauce on the side.

Variation Tip: You can add a lettuce leave to the filling as well.

Nutritional Information Per Serving: Calories 245 | Fat 14g |Sodium 122mg | Carbs 23.3g | Fiber 1.2g | Sugar 12g | Protein 4.3g

Apple Sandwich

Prep Time: 15 minutes | Cook Time: 5 minutes | Serves: 2

Ingredients:

4 slices whole-wheat bread, cut in 4-inch circle

½ teaspoons light butter

½ apple, sliced

1 tablespoon strawberry jam

Preparation:

1. Preheat the Breakfast Sandwich Maker until the green PREHEAT light comes on. Lift cover, top ring, and cooking plate. 2. Place a bread round in the bottom ring of the sandwich maker. 3. Spread ½ of the butter and jam on top. 4. Lower the cooking plate and top ring, then place ½ of the apple, and other bread slice on top. 5. Close the cover and cook for 5 minutes. Rotate the cooking plate handle clockwise until it stops. Then lift the cover and rings and carefully remove the sandwich with plastic spatula. 6. Repeat the same steps with the remaining ingredients. 7. Serve.

Serving Suggestion: Serve the sandwich with your favorite sauce on the side.

Variation Tip: You can add a drizzle of lemon juice on top of the filling as well.

Nutritional Information Per Serving: Calories 198 | Fat 14g |Sodium 272mg | Carbs 34g | Fiber 1g | Sugar 9.3g | Protein 1.3g

Honey Nuts Sandwich

Prep Time: 15 minutes | Cook Time: 10 minutes | Serves: 2

Ingredients:

4 slices whole-wheat bread, cut into 4-inch circle

½ teaspoon light butter

¼ cup roasted mixed nuts (almonds, pecans, walnuts, cashews,

etc.)

1 tablespoon wild honey

Preparation:

1. In a small bowl, mix together the mixed nuts and honey. 2. Preheat the Breakfast Sandwich Maker until the green PREHEAT light comes on. Lift cover, top ring, and cooking plate. 3. Lightly pat butter on each sandwich maker pan. 4. Place one bread slice, cut-side up, in bottom ring of the sandwich maker. 5. Lower the cooking plate and top ring. Add the nut mix to the cooking plate and top with a bread slice. 6. Close the cover and cook for 5 minutes. Rotate the cooking plate handle clockwise until it stops. Then lift the cover and rings and carefully remove the sandwich with plastic spatula. 7. Repeat the same steps with the remaining ingredients. 8. Serve.

Serving Suggestion: Serve the sandwich with coleslaw and your favorite sauce on the side.

Variation Tip: You can add a drizzle of paprika on top of the filling as well.

Nutritional Information Per Serving: Calories 173 | Fat 9.8g |Sodium 112.2mg | Carbs 17.5g | Fiber 1.2g | Sugar 12.2g | Protein 3.9g

Mango-Peach Sandwiches

Prep Time: 15 minutes | Cook Time: 10 minutes | Serves: 2

Ingredients:

4 slices whole-wheat bread, cut in 4-inch circle
½ teaspoon light butter
½ mango, sliced

1 peach, sliced
2 teaspoons pure maple syrup or wild honey

Preparation:

1. Spread the honey or maple syrup on each bread slice. 2. Preheat your Hamilton Beach Breakfast Sandwich Maker. 3. Lift the top cover, ring, and cooking plate. 4. Lightly pat butter on each sandwich maker pan. 5. Place one bread slice, cut-side up, in bottom ring of the sandwich maker. 6. Lower the cooking plate and top ring. Add half of mango and peach slices to the cooking plate and top with a bread slice. 7. Close the cover and cook for 5 minutes. Rotate the cooking plate handle clockwise until it stops. Then lift the cover and rings and carefully remove the sandwich with plastic spatula. 8. Repeat the same steps with the remaining ingredients. 9. Serve.

Serving Suggestion: Serve the sandwich with your favorite sauce on the side.

Variation Tip: Add some additional ground black pepper to the filling.

Nutritional Information Per Serving: Calories 297 | Fat 2.1g |Sodium 248.1mg | Carbs 64.9g | Fiber 3.9g | Sugar 9g | Protein 5.5g

Cheddar Apple Bacon Croissant

Prep Time: 15 minutes | Cook Time: 5 minutes | Serves: 2

Ingredients:

2 small croissants
2 large eggs
1 small Granny Smith apple

2 slices of precooked bacon
¼ cup of shredded cheddar cheese

Preparation:

1. Cut the apples into rounds, making sure to slice them very thinly. 2. Keep the peel as it is rich in nutrients. 3. Preheat the Breakfast Sandwich Maker until the green PREHEAT light comes on. Lift cover, top ring, and cooking plate. 4. Place half of the croissant in the bottom ring of the sandwich maker. 5. Top with ½ of the shredded cheddar cheese. 6. Place ½ of the apple slices and 1 slice of the precooked bacon on top, broken in half to make it fit on the croissant. 7. In a bowl, whisk the two eggs together. 8. Lower the cooking plate and top ring. Pour half of the egg into the cooking plate. 9. Then top with the other half of the croissant. 10. Close the cover and cook for 5 minutes. Rotate the cooking plate handle clockwise until it stops. Then lift the cover and rings and carefully remove the sandwich with plastic spatula. 11. Repeat the same steps with the remaining ingredients. 12. Serve.

Serving Suggestion: Serve the sandwich with your favorite sauce on the side.

Variation Tip: You can add a lettuce leave to the filling as well.

Nutritional Information Per Serving: Calories 251 | Fat 9g |Sodium 412mg | Carbs 43g | Fiber 5.3g | Sugar 1g | Protein 3g

Apricot and Brie Croissant

Prep Time: 15 minutes | Cook Time: 5 minutes | Serves: 1

Ingredients:

1 medium croissant
½ teaspoon of dark brown sugar
Cinnamon to taste

1 ounce of brie, cut into slices, rind removed
½ tablespoon of chopped, glazed pecans
1 tablespoon of apricot preserves

Preparation:

1. Preheat the Breakfast Sandwich Maker until the green PREHEAT light comes on. Lift cover, top ring, and cooking plate. 2. Place half of the croissant in the sandwich maker. 3. Lower the cooking plate and top ring. Place the cheese in the cooking plate. 4. Spread the apricot preserves on top and sprinkle with cinnamon, pecans, and sugar. 5. Then top with the other half of the croissant. 6. Close the cover and cook for 5 minutes. Rotate the cooking plate handle clockwise until it stops. Then lift the cover and rings and carefully remove the sandwich with plastic spatula. 7. Serve.

Serving Suggestion: Serve the sandwich with coleslaw and your favorite sauce on the side.

Variation Tip: You can add a lettuce leave to the filling as well.

Nutritional Information Per Serving: Calories 273| Fat 9.4g |Sodium 140mg | Carbs 47.2g | Fiber 1.9g | Sugar 30.4g | Protein 2.7g

Honey Pistachio Sandwich

Prep Time: 15 minutes | Cook Time: 10 minutes | Serves: 2

Ingredients:

4 slices whole-wheat bread, cut in 4-inch circle
½ teaspoons light butter
¼ cup pistachios, crushed

2 teaspoons wild honey
½ teaspoons ground cinnamon

Preparation:

1. In a small bowl, mix together the pistachios, cinnamon and wild honey. 2. Preheat the Breakfast Sandwich Maker until the green PREHEAT light comes on. Lift cover, top ring, and cooking plate. 3. Lightly pat butter on each sandwich maker pan. 4. Place one bread slice, in bottom ring of the sandwich maker. 5. Lower the cooking plate and top ring. Add half of the pistachios mixture to the cooking plate and top with a bread slice. 6. Close the cover and cook for 5 minutes. Rotate the cooking plate handle clockwise until it stops. Then lift the cover and rings and carefully remove the sandwich with plastic spatula. 7. Repeat the same steps with the remaining ingredients. 8. Serve.

Serving Suggestion: Serve the sandwich with crispy bacon and your favorite sauce on the side.

Variation Tip: You can add a layer of your favorite sauce to the filling as well.

Nutritional Information Per Serving: Calories 250 | Fat 13.6g | Sodium 99mg | Carbs 30.7g | Fiber 0.4g | Sugar 22.1g | Protein 2.4g

Dark Chocolate-Avocado Sandwich

Prep Time: 15 minutes | Cook Time: 10 minutes | Serves: 2

Ingredients:

4 slices whole-wheat bread, cut in 4-inch circle
½ teaspoons light butter
½ cup non-fat milk

1 small avocado, mashed
4 squares dark chocolate, 70% cocoa, slightly crushed

Preparation:

1. In a small bowl, mix together avocado, chocolate bits and milk. 2. Brush the bread slices with butter. 3. Preheat the Breakfast Sandwich Maker until the green PREHEAT light comes on. Lift cover, top ring, and cooking plate. 4. Place one bread slice, in bottom ring of the sandwich maker. 5. Lower the cooking plate and top ring. Add half of the chocolate-avocado mixture to the cooking plate and top with a bread slice. 6. Close the cover and cook for 5 minutes. Rotate the cooking plate handle clockwise until it stops. Then lift the cover and rings and carefully remove the sandwich with plastic spatula. 7. Repeat the same steps with the remaining ingredients. 8. Serve.

Serving Suggestion: Serve the sandwich with your favorite sauce on the side.

Variation Tip: Add some additional dried herbs to the filling.

Nutritional Information Per Serving: Calories 295 | Fat 3g | Sodium 355mg | Carbs 10g | Fiber 1g | Sugar 5g | Protein 1g

White Chocolate-Nut Sandwich

Prep Time: 15 minutes | Cook Time: 10 minutes | Serves: 2

Ingredients:

4 slices whole-wheat bread, cut in 4-inch circle
½ teaspoons light butter

¼ cup roasted macadamia nuts, chopped
6 squares white chocolate, slightly crushed

Preparation:

1. In a small bowl, mix together the macadamia chops and white chocolate bits. 2. Brush the bread slices with butter. 3. Preheat the Breakfast Sandwich Maker until the green PREHEAT light comes on. Lift cover, top ring, and cooking plate. 4. Place one bread slice, in bottom ring of the sandwich maker. 5. Lower the cooking plate and top ring. Add half of the nuts mixture to the cooking plate and top with a bread slice. 6. Close the cover and cook for 5 minutes. Rotate the cooking plate handle clockwise until it stops. Then lift the cover and rings and carefully remove the sandwich with plastic spatula. 7. Repeat the same steps with the remaining ingredients. 8. Serve.

Serving Suggestion: Serve the sandwich with crispy bacon and your favorite sauce on the side.

Variation Tip: Add some additional dried herbs to the filling.

Nutritional Information Per Serving: Calories 149 | Fat 1.2g |Sodium 3mg | Carbs 37.6g | Fiber 5.8g | Sugar 29g | Protein 1.1g

Mixed Fruit Sandwich

Prep time: 15 minutes | Cook Time: 10 minutes | Serves: 2

Ingredients:

4 whole wheat brown bread, cut into 4 inches' round
2 ripe bananas, peeled and sliced
2 pineapples, sliced thin

1 apple, sliced
2 tablespoon mixed fruit jam

Preparation:

1. Preheat the Breakfast Sandwich Maker until the green PREHEAT light comes on. Lift cover, top ring, and cooking plate. 2. Place a bread slice, inside the bottom ring of the sandwich maker. 3. Lower cooking plate and top ring. 4. Spread ½ of the apple, pineapple, jam and bananas in the cooking plate. 5. Top with the other bread slice. 6. Close the cover and cook for 5 minutes. Rotate the cooking plate handle clockwise until it stops. Then lift the cover and rings and carefully remove the sandwich with plastic spatula. 7. Repeat the same steps with the remaining ingredients. 8. Serve.
Serving Suggestion: Serve the sandwich with an avocado smoothie on the side.
Variation Tip: You can add a drizzle of sprinkles to the filling as well.
Nutritional Information Per Serving: Calories 282 | Fat 15g | Sodium 526mg | Carbs 20g | Fiber 0.6g | Sugar 3.3g | Protein 16g

Japanese Strawberry & Kiwi Sandwich

Prep time: 15 minutes | Cook Time: 10 minutes | Serves: 2

Ingredients:

12 strawberries, sliced
2 kiwis, sliced
1 navel orange, sliced
Whipped cream
1 cup heavy whipping cream
5 teaspoons sugar

4 slices shokupan (Japanese Pullman loaf bread), cut into 4 inches' round

1 teaspoon rum

Preparation:

1. In a small bowl, beat the cream with rum and sugar. 2. Preheat the Breakfast Sandwich Maker until the green PREHEAT light comes on. Lift cover, top ring, and cooking plate. 3. Place a bread slice inside the bottom ring of the sandwich maker. 4. Add half of the cream, orange, kiwi and strawberry. 5. Lower the cooking plate and top ring. Place the other bread slice inside. 6. Close the cover and cook for 5 minutes. Rotate the cooking plate handle clockwise until it stops. Then lift the cover and rings and carefully remove the sandwich with plastic spatula. 7. Repeat the same steps with the remaining ingredients. 8. Serve.
Serving Suggestion: Serve the sandwich with an apple smoothie on the side.
Variation Tip: You can add a drizzle of chocolate chips to the filling as well.
Nutritional Information Per Serving: Calories 284 | Fat 16g | Sodium 252mg | Carbs 31.6g | Fiber 0.9g | Sugar 6.6g | Protein 3.7g

Pumpkin-Apple Sandwich

Prep time: 15 minutes | Cook Time: 10 minutes | Serves: 2

Ingredients:

4 whole-wheat bread slices, cut into 4 inches' round
2 tablespoon pumpkin puree
1 apple, sliced

2 pinches pumpkin pie spice
2 tablespoon applesauce

Preparation:

1. Preheat the Breakfast Sandwich Maker until the green PREHEAT light comes on. Lift cover, top ring, and cooking plate. 2. Place a bread slice, inside the bottom ring of the sandwich maker. 3. Spread ½ of the applesauce, pumpkin puree, a pinch of spice and apple on top. 4. Lower cooking plate and top ring. Place the other bread slice inside. 5. Close the cover and cook for 5 minutes. Rotate the cooking plate handle clockwise until it stops. Then lift the cover and rings and carefully remove the sandwich with plastic spatula. 6. Repeat the same steps with the remaining ingredients. 7. Serve.
Serving Suggestion: Serve the sandwich with a broccoli salad on the side.
Variation Tip: You can add a drizzle of chocolate syrup to the filling as well.
Nutritional Information Per Serving: Calories 282 | Fat 15g | Sodium 526mg | Carbs 20g | Fiber 0.6g | Sugar 3.3g | Protein 16g

Apple Raisin Sandwich

Prep Time: 15 minutes | Cook Time: 5 minutes | Serves: 1

Ingredients:

1 cinnamon raisin bagel

½ medium granny smith apple, sliced

1 slice of sharp cheddar cheese

Preparation:

1. Preheat your Hamilton Beach Breakfast Sandwich Maker. 2. Lift the top cover, ring, and cooking plate. 3. Place the lower half of the bagel in the sandwich maker. 4. Top the bottom of the bagel with the thin slices of apple. 5. Place the slice of sharp cheddar cheese on top of the apple slices. 6. Now lower the cooking plate and top rings. 7. Place the other top half of the bagel on top. 8. Cover the top hood, and let the sandwich cook for 5 minutes. 9. When finished cooking, rotate the handle of the cooking plate clockwise until it stops. 10. Lift the hood, the rings and transfer the sandwich to a plate. 11. Serve.

Serving Suggestion: Serve the sandwich with coleslaw and your favorite sauce on the side.

Variation Tip: You can add a lettuce leave to the filling as well.

Nutritional Information Per Serving: Calories 284 | Fat 16g |Sodium 252mg | Carbs 31.6g | Fiber 0.9g | Sugar 6.6g | Protein 3.7g

Ricotta Cheese Nectarine Biscuit

Prep Time: 15 minutes | Cook Time: 5 minutes | Serves: 1

Ingredients:

1 buttermilk biscuit, sliced

1 ripe nectarine, peeled and sliced

1 tablespoon ricotta cheese

1 tablespoon maple syrup

2 teaspoons brown sugar

Preparation:

1. Preheat your Hamilton Beach Breakfast Sandwich Maker. 2. Lift the top cover, ring, and cooking plate. 3. Place the lower half of the biscuit in the sandwich maker. 4. Place the nectarines in a bowl and add the ricotta, maple syrup and brown sugar then toss well. 5. Top the biscuit with the nectarine slices, ricotta, maple syrup and brown sugar mixture. 6. Place the other top half of the biscuit on top of the nectarines. 7. Now lower the cooking plate and top rings. 8. Cover the top hood, and let the sandwich cook for 5 minutes. 9. When finished cooking, rotate the handle of the cooking plate clockwise until it stops. 10. Lift the hood, the rings and transfer the sandwich to a plate. 11. Serve.

Serving Suggestion: Serve the sandwich with your favorite sauce on the side.

Variation Tip: Add some additional ground black pepper to the filling.

Nutritional Information Per Serving: Calories 391 | Fat 24g |Sodium 142mg | Carbs 38.5g | Fiber 3.5g | Sugar 21g | Protein 6.6g

Bacon-Avocado Cheese Sandwich

Prep Time: 15 minutes | Cook Time: 5 minutes | Serves: 1

Ingredients:

2 slices multi-grain bread, cut in 4-inch circle

2 slices thick cut bacon, cooked

1 slice sharp cheddar

¼ avocado, sliced

1 slice red onion

1 tablespoon Aioli

1 large egg

Preparation:

1. Preheat your Hamilton Beach Breakfast Sandwich Maker. 2. Lift the top cover, ring, and cooking plate. 3. Place one bread slice in the sandwich maker and top it with bacon, avocado, onion and aioli. 4. Now lower the cooking plate and top rings, then pour in the egg. 5. Add the cheese and other circle of the bread on top. 6. Cover the top hood, and let the sandwich cook for 5 minutes. 7. When finished cooking, rotate the handle of the cooking plate clockwise until it stops. 8. Lift the hood, the rings and transfer the sandwich to a plate. 9. Serve.

Serving Suggestion: Serve the sandwich with your favorite sauce on the side.

Variation Tip: You can add a lettuce leave to the filling as well.

Nutritional Information Per Serving: Calories 327 | Fat 14.2g |Sodium 672mg | Carbs 47.2g | Fiber 1.7g | Sugar 24.8g | Protein 4.4g

Nutella-Avocado Cheese Sandwich

Prep time: 15 minutes | Cook Time: 5 minutes | Serves: 2

Ingredients:

4 whole-wheat bread slices, cut into 4 inches' round
2 tablespoon Nutella spread

1 avocado, sliced
2 tablespoon cream cheese

Preparation:

1. Preheat your Hamilton Beach Breakfast Sandwich Maker until PREHEAT light gets green. 2. Lift the top cover, ring, and cooking plate. 3. Place a bread slice, inside the bottom tray of the sandwich maker. 4. Spread ½ of the cream cheese, Nutella and avocado on top. 5. Place the other bread slice on top. 6. Now lower the cooking plate and top rings then. 7. Cover the top hood, and let the sandwich cook for 5 minutes. 8. Rotate the handle of the cooking plate clockwise until it stops. 9. Lift the hood, the rings and transfer the sandwich to a plate. 10. Repeat the same steps with the remaining ingredients. 11. Serve.

Serving Suggestion: Serve the sandwich with a glass of chocolate smoothie on the side.

Variation Tip: You can add a drizzle of chocolate chips to the filling as well.

Nutritional Information Per Serving: Calories 282 | Fat 15g |Sodium 526mg | Carbs 20g | Fiber 0.6g | Sugar 3.3g | Protein 16g

Nutella Raspberry Cheese Sandwich

Prep time: 15 minutes | Cook Time: 5 minutes | Serves: 2

Ingredients:

4 brown bread slices, cut into 4 inches' round
2 tablespoon Nutella spread
½ fresh raspberries, sliced

2 tablespoon raspberry preserves
2 tablespoons cream cheese

Preparation:

1. Preheat your Hamilton Beach Breakfast Sandwich Maker until PREHEAT light gets green. 2. Lift the top cover, ring, and cooking plate. 3. Place a bread slice, inside the bottom tray of the sandwich maker. 4. Spread ½ of the preserves, Nutella, raspberries and cream cheese on top. 5. Place the other bread slice on top. 6. Now lower the cooking plate and top rings then. 7. Cover the top hood, and let the sandwich cook for 5 minutes. 8. Rotate the handle of the cooking plate clockwise until it stops. 9. Lift the hood, the rings and transfer the sandwich to a plate. 10. Repeat the same steps with the remaining ingredients. 11. Serve.

Serving Suggestion: Serve the sandwich with a banana smoothie on the side.

Variation Tip: You can add a drizzle of chocolate chips to the filling as well.

Nutritional Information Per Serving: Calories 282 | Fat 15g |Sodium 526mg | Carbs 20g | Fiber 0.6g | Sugar 3.3g | Protein 16g

Apple Nutella Sandwich

Prep time: 15 minutes | Cook Time: 5 minutes | Serves: 2

Ingredients:

4 brown bread slices, cut into 4 inches' round
2 tablespoon Nutella spread

1 apple, sliced
2 tablespoon jam

Preparation:

1. Preheat your Hamilton Beach Breakfast Sandwich Maker until PREHEAT light gets green. 2. Lift the top cover, ring, and cooking plate. 3. Place a bread slice, inside the bottom tray of the sandwich maker. 4. Spread ½ of the jam, Nutella and apple on top. 5. Now lower the cooking plate and top rings then. 6. Place the other bread slice on top. 7. Cover the top hood, and let the sandwich cook for 5 minutes. 8. Rotate the handle of the cooking plate clockwise until it stops. 9. Lift the hood, the rings and transfer the sandwich to a plate. 10. Repeat the same steps with the remaining ingredients. 11. Serve.

Serving Suggestion: Serve the sandwich with a glass of green smoothie on the side.

Variation Tip: You can add a drizzle of chocolate syrup to the filling as well.

Nutritional Information Per Serving: Calories 282 | Fat 15g |Sodium 526mg | Carbs 20g | Fiber 0.6g | Sugar 3.3g | Protein 16g

Delicious Peach Bran Sandwich

Prep time: 15 minutes | Cook Time: 5 minutes | Serves: 2

Ingredients:

4 bran bread slices, cut into 4 inches' round
2 tablespoon peach preserves

1 peach, peeled and sliced

Preparation:

1. Preheat your Hamilton Beach Breakfast Sandwich Maker until PREHEAT light gets green. 2. Lift the top cover, ring, and cooking plate. 3. Place a bread slice, inside the bottom tray of the sandwich maker. 4. Spread ½ of the preserves, and peach slices on top. 5. Now lower the cooking plate and top rings then. 6. Place the other bread slice on top. 7. Cover the top hood, and let the sandwich cook for 5 minutes. 8. Rotate the handle of the cooking plate clockwise until it stops. 9. Lift the hood, the rings and transfer the sandwich to a plate. 10. Repeat the same steps with the remaining ingredients. 11. Serve.

Serving Suggestion: Serve the sandwich with a glass of orange juice on the side.

Variation Tip: You can add a drizzle of chocolate chips to the filling as well.

Nutritional Information Per Serving: Calories 282 | Fat 15g |Sodium 526mg | Carbs 20g | Fiber 0.6g | Sugar 3.3g | Protein 16g

Chocolate-Hazelnut Banana Sandwich

Prep time: 15 minutes | Cook Time: 5 minutes | Serves: 4

Ingredients:

8 banana bread slices, cut into 4 inches' round
4 tablespoon cream cheese
4 tablespoons chocolate-hazelnut spread

4 tablespoons peanut butter
2 bananas, sliced

Preparation:

1. Preheat your Hamilton Beach Breakfast Sandwich Maker until PREHEAT light gets green. 2. Lift the top cover, ring, and cooking plate. 3. Place a bread slice, inside the bottom tray of the sandwich maker. 4. Spread 1/4 of the cream cheese, chocolate spread, peanut butter and bananas on top. 5. Now lower the cooking plate and top rings. 6. Place the other bread slice on top. 7. Cover the top hood, and let the sandwich cook for 5 minutes. 8. Rotate the handle of the cooking plate clockwise until it stops. 9. Lift the hood, the rings and transfer the sandwich to a plate. 10. Repeat the same steps with the remaining ingredients. 11. Serve.

Serving Suggestion: Serve the sandwich with an apple smoothie on the side.

Variation Tip: You can add a drizzle of chocolate chips to the filling as well.

Nutritional Information Per Serving: Calories 282 | Fat 15g |Sodium 526mg | Carbs 20g | Fiber 0.6g | Sugar 3.3g | Protein 16g

Nutella Blueberry Sandwich

Prep time: 15 minutes | Cook Time: 5 minutes | Serves: 2

Ingredients:

4 white bread slices, cut into 4 inches' round
2 tablespoon Nutella spread

½ fresh blueberries, sliced
2 tablespoon blueberry preserves

Preparation:

1. Preheat your Hamilton Beach Breakfast Sandwich Maker until PREHEAT light gets green. 2. Lift the top cover, ring, and cooking plate. 3. Place a bread slice, inside the bottom tray of the sandwich maker. 4. Spread ½ of the preserves, Nutella and blueberries on top. 5. Now lower the cooking plate and top rings then. 6. Place the other bread slice on top. 7. Cover the top hood, and let the sandwich cook for 5 minutes. 8. Rotate the handle of the cooking plate clockwise until it stops. 9. Lift the hood, the rings and transfer the sandwich to a plate. 10. Repeat the same steps with the remaining ingredients. 11. Serve.

Serving Suggestion: Serve the sandwich with a chocolate smoothie on the side.

Variation Tip: You can add a drizzle of chocolate sprinkles to the filling as well.

Nutritional Information Per Serving: Calories 282 | Fat 15g |Sodium 526mg | Carbs 20g | Fiber 0.6g | Sugar 3.3g | Protein 16g

Dark Chocolate Cherry Sandwich

Prep Time: 15 minutes | Cook Time: 5 minutes | Serves: 2

Ingredients:

4 slices whole-wheat bread, cut in 4-inch circle
½ teaspoons light butter

¼ cup cherries, slightly crushed
6 squares dark chocolate 70% cocoa, slightly crushed

Preparation:

1. Mix together the cherries and dark chocolate. 2. Make two sandwiches with the chocolate and cherry mixture. 3. Preheat your Hamilton Beach Breakfast Sandwich Maker. 4. Lift the top cover, ring, and cooking plate. 5. Lightly pat butter on each sandwich maker pan. 6. Place a sandwich in the sandwich maker. 7. Now lower the cooking plate and top rings. 8. Cover the top hood, and let the sandwich cook for 5 minutes. 9. When finished cooking, rotate the handle of the cooking plate clockwise until it stops. 10. Lift the hood, the rings and transfer the sandwich to a plate. 11. Repeat the same steps with the remaining ingredients. 12. Serve.
Serving Suggestion: Serve the sandwich with crispy bacon and your favorite sauce on the side.
Variation Tip: Add some additional dried herbs to the filling.
Nutritional Information Per Serving: Calories 186| Fat 9 g | Sodium 124mg | Carbs 23 g | Fiber 0.4g | Sugar 11.5 g | Protein 3.2 g

Homemade Peanut Butter Banana Sandwich

Prep Time: 15 minutes | Cook Time: 5 minutes | Serves: 2

Ingredients:

4 slices whole-wheat bread, cut in 4-inch circle
½ teaspoons light butter

1 medium banana, slightly crushed
1 tablespoon peanut butter

Preparation:

1. Make two sandwiches, layering peanut butter spread and crushed bananas. 2. Preheat your Hamilton Beach Breakfast Sandwich Maker. 3. Lift the top cover, ring, and cooking plate. 4. Lightly pat butter on each sandwich maker pan. 5. Place a sandwich in the sandwich maker. 6. Now lower the cooking plate and top rings. 7. Cover the top hood, and let the sandwich cook for 5 minutes. 8. When finished cooking, rotate the handle of the cooking plate clockwise until it stops. 9. Lift the hood, the rings and transfer the sandwich to a plate. 10. Repeat the same steps with the remaining ingredients. 11. Serve hot.
Serving Suggestion: Serve the sandwich with your favorite sauce on the side.
Variation Tip: Add some additional ground black pepper to the filling.
Nutritional Information Per Serving: Calories 121 | Fat 7.1 g | Sodium 110mg | Carbs 5 g | Fiber 0.5g | Sugar 1.1 g | Protein 10 g

Strawberry Nutella Sandwich

Prep time: 15 minutes | Cook Time: 5 minutes | Serves: 2

Ingredients:

4 white bread slices, cut into 4 inches' round
2 tablespoon Nutella spread

½ fresh strawberries, sliced
2 tablespoon strawberry jam

Preparation:

1. Preheat your Hamilton Beach Breakfast Sandwich Maker until PREHEAT light gets green. 2. Lift the top cover, ring, and cooking plate. 3. Place a bread slice, inside the bottom tray of the sandwich maker. 4. Spread ½ of the jam, Nutella and strawberry on top. 5. Now lower the cooking plate and top rings then. 6. Place the other bread slice on top. 7. Cover the top hood, and let the sandwich cook for 5 minutes. 8. Rotate the handle of the cooking plate clockwise until it stops. 9. Lift the hood, the rings and transfer the sandwich to a plate. 10. Repeat the same steps with the remaining ingredients. 11. Serve.
Serving Suggestion: Serve the sandwich with a banana smoothie on the side.
Variation Tip: You can add a drizzle of chocolate chips to the filling as well.
Nutritional Information Per Serving: Calories 282 | Fat 15g |Sodium 526mg | Carbs 20g | Fiber 0.6g | Sugar 3.3g | Protein 16g

Cinnamon Apple Sandwich

Prep Time: 15 minutes | Cook Time: 5 minutes | Serves: 2

Ingredients:

4 slices whole-wheat bread, cut in 4-inch circle
½ teaspoons light butter
½ apple, sliced

1 teaspoon ground cinnamon
2 teaspoons pure maple syrup

Preparation:

1. Spread maple syrup on each bread slice. 2. Make two sandwiches, layering apple slices, and sprinkles of cinnamon powder. 3. Preheat your Hamilton Beach Breakfast Sandwich Maker. 4. Lift the top cover, ring, and cooking plate. Lightly pat butter on each sandwich maker pan. 5. Place a sandwich in the sandwich maker. 6. Now lower the cooking plate and top rings. 7. Cover the top hood, and let the sandwich cook for 5 minutes. 8. When finished cooking, rotate the handle of the cooking plate clockwise until it stops. 9. Lift the hood, the rings and transfer the sandwich to a plate. 10. Repeat the same steps with the remaining ingredients. 11. Serve.

Serving Suggestion: Serve the sandwich with crispy bacon and your favorite sauce on the side.

Variation Tip: Add some additional dried herbs to the filling.

Nutritional Information Per Serving: Calories 266 | Fat 11.8g |Sodium 267mg | Carbs 37.6g | Fiber 2.3g | Sugar 5g | Protein 2.2g

Chapter 8 Snacks and Desserts Sandwich

78 Mini Vanilla Cake

78 Taleggio Cheese Ham Sandwich

78 Cheese Apple Ham Panini

79 Tasty Nutella Banana Panini

79 Cheese Apple Pie Panini

79 Fresh Strawberry English Muffin Pies

80 Banana Chocolate Chip Panini

80 Brie Strawberry Muffin Sandwich

80 Raspberry English Muffin Pies

81 Cheese Spinach and Avocado Panini

81 Brie Cheese Chocolate Panini

81 Blueberry Muffin Hand Pies

82 Nutella Cinnamon Quesadilla

82 Brie Cheese Raspberry Sandwiches

82 Chocolate Marshmallow Banana Sandwiches

83 Pumpkin Butter Chocolate Brie Sandwich

83 Dark Chocolate Pomegranate Sandwich

83 Strawberry Marshmallow Panini

84 Cranberry Turkey-Bacon Panini

84 Chicken Tomato Guacamole Panini

84 Balsamic Mato Panini

85 Chocolate Marshmallow Panini

85 Chocolate Raspberry Cream Cheese Panini

85 Dark Chocolate-Raspberry Sandwiches

86 Kanafeh Pistachios Cheese Sandwich

Mini Vanilla Cake

Prep Time: 15 minutes | Cook Time: 5 minutes | Serves: 1

Ingredients:

1 egg
3 tablespoons sugar
2 tablespoons milk
¼ cup cooking oil/butter

½ teaspoon vanilla essence
½ cup all-purpose flour/ maida
½ teaspoon baking powder

Preparation:

1. Add egg and sugar in a bowl and whisk until mixture changes color and fluff up. 2. Now add milk, vanilla essence and oil in the egg mixture and whisk again to combine everything. 3. Add in all-purpose flour, baking powder and fold everything well with a spatula. 4. Preheat your Hamilton Beach Breakfast Sandwich Maker. 5. Lift the top cover, ring, and cooking plate. 6. Now lower the cooking plate and top rings then pour in the prepared batter. 7. Cover the top hood, and let the sandwich cook for 5 minutes. 8. When finished cooking, rotate the handle of the cooking plate clockwise until it stops. 9. Lift the hood, the rings and transfer the sandwich to a plate. 10. Serve.
Serving Suggestion: Serve the sandwich with coleslaw and your favorite sauce on the side.
Variation Tip: You can add a drizzle of lemon juice on top of the filling as well.
Nutritional Information Per Serving: Calories 192 | Fat 9.3g |Sodium 133mg | Carbs 27.1g | Fiber 1.4g | Sugar 19g | Protein 3.2g

Taleggio Cheese Ham Sandwich

Prep Time: 15 minutes | Cook Time: 5 minutes | Serves: 2

Ingredients:

4 slices of sandwich bread, cut in 4-inch circle
6 teaspoons butter soft

4 tablespoons Taleggio cheese - rind removed
2 ham slices, grilled

Preparation:

1. Preheat your Hamilton Beach Breakfast Sandwich Maker. 2. Lift the top cover, ring, and cooking plate. 3. Place one bread slice in the sandwich maker and top it with butter. 4. Now lower the cooking plate and top rings then add ½ of the cheese and ham. 5. Add the other circle of the bread on top. 6. Cover the top hood, and let the sandwich cook for 5 minutes. 7. When finished cooking, rotate the handle of the cooking plate clockwise until it stops. 8. Lift the hood, the rings and transfer the sandwich to a plate. 9. Repeat the same steps with the remaining ingredients. 10. Serve.
Serving Suggestion: Serve the sandwich with your favorite sauce on the side.
Variation Tip: Add some additional ground black pepper to the filling.
Nutritional Information Per Serving: Calories 305 | Fat 25g |Sodium 532mg | Carbs 2.3g | Fiber 0.4g | Sugar 2g | Protein 18.3g

Cheese Apple Ham Panini

Prep Time: 15 minutes | Cook Time: 5 minutes | Serves: 4

Ingredients:

8 slices multigrain bread, cut in 4-inch circle
2 tablespoons mayonnaise
2 tablespoons Dijon mustard
4 tablespoons butter softened

8 ounces thick-sliced ham pieces
1 small apple cored and thinly sliced
8-ounce Swiss cheese grated

Preparation:

1. Preheat your Hamilton Beach Breakfast Sandwich Maker. 2. Lift the top cover, ring, and cooking plate. 3. Place a bread slice in the sandwich maker and top with ¼th of the mayo, mustard and butter. 4. Now lower the cooking plate and top rings, then add ¼th of the apple, ham and cheese. 5. Add the other circle of the bread on top. 6. Cover the top hood, and let the sandwich cook for 5 minutes. 7. When finished cooking, rotate the handle of the cooking plate clockwise until it stops. 8. Lift the hood, the rings and transfer the sandwich to a plate. 9. Repeat the same steps with the remaining ingredients. 10. Serve.
Serving Suggestion: Serve the sandwich with crispy bacon and your favorite sauce on the side.
Variation Tip: Add some additional ground black pepper to the filling.
Nutritional Information Per Serving: Calories 229 | Fat 1.9 |Sodium 567mg | Carbs 1.9g | Fiber 0.4g | Sugar 0.6g | Protein 11.8g

Tasty Nutella Banana Panini

Prep Time: 15 minutes | Cook Time: 5 minutes | Serves: 2

Ingredients:

4 slices French bread, cut in 4-inch circle
6 tablespoons Nutella spread
6 tablespoons Marshmallow cream

1 large banana sliced
2-3 tablespoons butter

Preparation:

1. Preheat your Hamilton Beach Breakfast Sandwich Maker. 2. Lift the top cover, ring, and cooking plate. 3. Place one bread slice in the sandwich maker and top it with ½ of butter, spread, and cream. 4. Now lower the cooking plate and top rings then add ½ of the banana. 5. Add the other circle of the bread on top. 6. Cover the top hood, and let the sandwich cook for 5 minutes. 7. When finished cooking, rotate the handle of the cooking plate clockwise until it stops. 8. Lift the hood, the rings and transfer the sandwich to a plate. 9. Repeat the same steps with the remaining ingredients. 10. Serve.
Serving Suggestion: Serve the sandwich with crispy bacon and your favorite sauce on the side.
Variation Tip: Add some additional dried herbs to the filling.
Nutritional Information Per Serving: Calories 190 | Fat 18g |Sodium 150mg | Carbs 0.6g | Fiber 0.4g | Sugar 0.4g | Protein 7.2g

Cheese Apple Pie Panini

Prep Time: 15 minutes | Cook Time: 5 minutes | Serves: 4

Ingredients:

½ cup mascarpone cheese
2 teaspoons honey
4 tablespoons (½ stick) butter

8 slices cinnamon raisin bread, cut in 4-inch circle
1 Granny Smith apple, cored and sliced
2 tablespoons light brown sugar

Preparation:

1. Blend mascarpone cheese with honey, sugar and butter. 2. Preheat your Hamilton Beach Breakfast Sandwich Maker. 3. Lift the top cover, ring, and cooking plate. 4. Place one bread slice in the sandwich maker and top it with ¼ cheese mixture. 5. Now lower the cooking plate and top rings then add ¼ apples on top. 6. Add the other circle of the bread on top. 7. Cover the top hood, and let the sandwich cook for 5 minutes. 8. When finished cooking, rotate the handle of the cooking plate clockwise until it stops. 9. Lift the hood, the rings and transfer the sandwich to a plate. 10. Repeat the same steps with the remaining ingredients. 11. Serve.
Serving Suggestion: Serve the sandwich with your favorite sauce on the side.
Variation Tip: You can add a lettuce leave to the filling as well.
Nutritional Information Per Serving: Calories 183 | Fat 15g |Sodium 402mg | Carbs 2.5g | Fiber 0.4g | Sugar 1.1g | Protein 10g

Fresh Strawberry English Muffin Pies

Prep time: 15 minutes | Cook Time: 12 minutes | Serves: 6

Ingredients:

6 English muffins, cut in half
½ cup sugar
3 tablespoons cornstarch
½ teaspoon ground cinnamon
1 teaspoon lemon zest
1 tablespoon fresh lemon juice

2 ½ cups fresh strawberries
A pinch of salt
1 egg yolk
2 tablespoons of water
Sugar, for sprinkling

Preparation:

1. Mix strawberries with salt, lemon juice, zest, cinnamon, sugar and cornstarch in a saucepan. 2. Stir and cook berries on low heat for 5-7 minutes. 3. Allow this berry filling to cool at room temperature. 4. Preheat your Hamilton Beach Breakfast Sandwich Maker until PREHEAT light gets green. 5. Lift the top cover, ring, and cooking plate. 6. Place half of a muffin inside the bottom tray of the sandwich maker. 7. Add a tablespoon of berry filing to its center. 8. Place the other top half of the muffin on top. 9. Now lower the cooking plate and top rings. 10. Cover the top hood, and let the sandwich cook for 5 minutes. 11. Rotate the handle of the cooking plate clockwise until it stops. 12. Lift the hood, the rings and transfer the sandwich to a plate. 13. Make more berry pies in the same way. 14. Serve.
Serving Suggestion: Serve the pie with an apple smoothie on the side.
Variation Tip: you can add some mascarpone to the filling as well.
Nutritional Information Per Serving: Calories 351 | Fat 19g |Sodium 412mg | Carbs 13g | Fiber 0.3g | Sugar 1g | Protein 23g

Banana Chocolate Chip Panini

Prep Time: 15 minutes | Cook Time: 5 minutes | Serves: 1

Ingredients:

2 slices whole-grain bread, cut in 4-inch circle

2 tablespoons natural peanut or almond butter (no added salt or sugar)

10 bittersweet chocolate chips (60% cocoa)

½ banana, sliced

Preparation:

1. Preheat your Hamilton Beach Breakfast Sandwich Maker. 2. Lift the top cover, ring, and cooking plate. 3. Place one bread slice in the sandwich maker and top it with peanut butter and chocolate chips. 4. Now lower the cooking plate and top rings, then add banana. 5. Add the other circle of the bread on top. 6. Cover the top hood, and let the sandwich cook for 5 minutes. 7. When finished cooking, rotate the handle of the cooking plate clockwise until it stops. 8. Lift the hood, the rings and transfer the sandwich to a plate. 9. Serve.

Serving Suggestion: Serve the sandwich with coleslaw and your favorite sauce on the side.

Variation Tip: You can add a drizzle of paprika on top of the filling as well.

Nutritional Information Per Serving: Calories 267 | Fat 12g |Sodium 165mg | Carbs 39g | Fiber 1.4g | Sugar 22g | Protein 3.3g

Brie Strawberry Muffin Sandwich

Prep Time: 15 minutes | Cook Time: 5 minutes | Serves: 1

Ingredients:

1 ounce brie, rind removed, and sliced

1 English muffins, cut in half

1 ounce sliced smoked turkey

1 fresh basil leaves, sliced

2 tablespoons sliced strawberries

½ tablespoon pepper jelly

½ tablespoon butter, melted

Preparation:

1. Preheat your Hamilton Beach Breakfast Sandwich Maker. 2. Lift the top cover, ring, and cooking plate. 3. Place the lower half of the muffin in the sandwich maker and top it with butter and brie. 4. Now lower the cooking plate and top rings, then add turkey and rest of the fillings. 5. Place another muffin half on top. 6. Cover the top hood, and let the sandwich cook for 5 minutes. 7. When finished cooking, rotate the handle of the cooking plate clockwise until it stops. 8. Lift the hood, the rings and transfer the sandwich to a plate. 9. Serve.

Serving Suggestion: Serve the sandwich with crispy bacon and your favorite sauce on the side.

Variation Tip: Add some additional ground black pepper to the filling.

Nutritional Information Per Serving: Calories 102 | Fat 7.6g |Sodium 545mg | Carbs 1.5g | Fiber 0.4g | Sugar 0.7g | Protein 7.1g

Raspberry English Muffin Pies

Prep time: 15 minutes | Cook Time: 12 minutes | Serves: 6

Ingredients:

½ cup sugar

3 tablespoons cornstarch

½ teaspoon ground cinnamon

1 teaspoon lemon zest

6 English muffin

1 tablespoon fresh lemon juice

2 ½ cups fresh raspberries

A pinch of salt

1 egg yolk

2 tablespoons of water

Sugar, for sprinkling

Preparation:

1. Mix raspberries with salt, lemon juice, zest, cinnamon, sugar and cornstarch in a saucepan. 2. Stir and cook berries on low heat for 5-7 minutes. 3. Allow this berry filling to cool at room temperature. 4. Preheat your Hamilton Beach Breakfast Sandwich Maker until PREHEAT light gets green. 5. Lift the top cover, ring, and cooking plate. 6. Place half of a muffin inside the bottom tray of the sandwich maker. 7. Add a tablespoon of berry filing to its center. 8. Place the other top half of the muffin on top. 9. Now lower the cooking plate and top rings. 10. Cover the top hood, and let the sandwich cook for 5 minutes. 11. Rotate the handle of the cooking plate clockwise until it stops. 12. Lift the hood, the rings and transfer the sandwich to a plate. 13. Make more berry pies in the same way. 14. Serve.

Serving Suggestion: Serve the pie with a banana smoothie on the side.

Variation Tip: you can add some extra cream to the filling as well.

Nutritional Information Per Serving: Calories 351 | Fat 19g |Sodium 412mg | Carbs 13g | Fiber 0.3g | Sugar 1g | Protein 23g

Cheese Spinach and Avocado Panini

Prep Time: 15 minutes | Cook Time: 5 minutes | Serves: 1

Ingredients:

2 sourdough bread slices, cut in 4-inch circle
1 tablespoon light mayo
1 tablespoon butter
1 slice Colby jack cheese

6 leaves spinach
2 slices tomatoes
½ avocado sliced

Preparation:

1. Preheat your Hamilton Beach Breakfast Sandwich Maker. 2. Lift the top cover, ring, and cooking plate. 3. Place one bread slice in the sandwich maker and top it with mayo, butter, spinach. 4. Now lower the cooking plate and top rings, then add avocado, tomato and cheese. 5. Add the other circle of the bread on top. 6. Cover the top hood, and let the sandwich cook for 5 minutes. 7. When finished cooking, rotate the handle of the cooking plate clockwise until it stops. 8. Lift the hood, the rings and transfer the sandwich to a plate. 9. Serve.

Serving Suggestion: Serve the sandwich with your favorite sauce on the side.

Variation Tip: Add some additional dried herbs to the filling.

Nutritional Information Per Serving: Calories 237 | Fat 19g |Sodium 518mg | Carbs 7g | Fiber 1.5g | Sugar 3.4g | Protein 12g

Brie Cheese Chocolate Panini

Prep Time: 15 minutes | Cook Time: 5 minutes | Serves: 2

Ingredients:

4 slices crunchy sourdough bread, cut in 4-inch circle
4 ounces Brie cheese, cut into slices

2-ounces milk chocolate
2 tablespoons unsalted butter, melted

Preparation:

1. Preheat your Hamilton Beach Breakfast Sandwich Maker. 2. Lift the top cover, ring, and cooking plate. 3. Place one bread slice in the sandwich maker and top it with ½ of the butter, brie and chocolate. 4. Now lower the cooking plate and top rings. 5. Add the other circle of the bread on top. 6. Cover the top hood, and let the sandwich cook for 5 minutes. 7. When finished cooking, rotate the handle of the cooking plate clockwise until it stops. 8. Lift the hood, the rings and transfer the sandwich to a plate. 9. Repeat the same steps with the remaining ingredients. 10. Serve.

Serving Suggestion: Serve the sandwich with your favorite sauce on the side.

Variation Tip: You can add a lettuce leave to the filling as well.

Nutritional Information Per Serving: Calories 209 | Fat 7.5g |Sodium 321mg | Carbs 34.1g | Fiber 4g | Sugar 3.8g | Protein 4.3g

Blueberry Muffin Hand Pies

Prep time: 15 minutes | Cook Time: 12 minutes | Serves: 6

Ingredients:

6 English muffins, cut in half
½ cup sugar
3 tablespoons cornstarch
½ teaspoon ground cinnamon
1 teaspoon lemon zest
1 tablespoon fresh lemon juice

2 ½ cups fresh blueberries
A pinch of salt
1 egg yolk
2 tablespoons of water
Sugar, for sprinkling

Preparation:

1. Mix blueberries with salt, lemon juice, zest, cinnamon, sugar and cornstarch in a saucepan. 2. Stir and cook berries on low heat for 5-7 minutes. 3. Allow this berry filling to cool at room temperature. 4. Preheat your Hamilton Beach Breakfast Sandwich Maker until PREHEAT light gets green. 5. Lift the top cover, ring, and cooking plate. 6. Place half of a muffin inside the bottom tray of the sandwich maker. 7. Add ⅙ egg yolk and a tablespoon of berry filing to its center. 8. Place the other top half of the muffin on top. 9. Now lower the cooking plate and top rings. 10. Cover the top hood, and let the sandwich cook for 5 minutes. 11. Rotate the handle of the cooking plate clockwise until it stops. 12. Lift the hood, the rings and transfer the sandwich to a plate. 13. Make more berry pies in the same way. 14. Serve.

Serving Suggestion: Serve the pies with chocolate sauce on the side.

Variation Tip: You can add chocolate chips to the filling as well.

Nutritional Information Per Serving: Calories 351 | Fat 19g |Sodium 412mg | Carbs 13g | Fiber 0.3g | Sugar 1g | Protein 23g

Nutella Cinnamon Quesadilla

Prep time: 15 minutes | Cook Time: 5 minutes | Serves: 1

Ingredients:

¼ cup granulated sugar
1 tablespoon cinnamon
1 tablespoon butter

1 (10 inches) flour tortilla, cut into two 4 inches' rounds
2-3 tablespoons Nutella

Preparation:

1. Preheat your Hamilton Beach Breakfast Sandwich Maker until PREHEAT light gets green. 2. Lift the top cover, ring, and cooking plate. 3. Place a tortilla round inside the bottom tray of the sandwich maker. 4. Spread Nutella, cinnamon, sugar and butter on top. 5. Now lower the cooking plate and top rings. 6. Place a tortilla round on top. 7. Cover the top hood, and let the sandwich cook for 5 minutes. 8. Rotate the handle of the cooking plate clockwise until it stops. 9. Lift the hood, the rings and transfer the sandwich to a plate. 10. Serve.

Serving Suggestion: Serve the quesadilla with a banana smoothie on the side.

Variation Tip: you can add some crushed crackers to the filling as well.

Nutritional Information Per Serving: Calories 256 | Fat 4g |Sodium 634mg | Carbs 33g | Fiber 1.4g | Sugar 1g | Protein 3g

Brie Cheese Raspberry Sandwiches

Prep time: 15 minutes | Cook Time: 5 minutes | Serves: 2

Ingredients:

8 ounces brie cheese
12 ounces semi-sweet chocolate

12 ounces fresh raspberries
2 English muffins split in half

Preparation:

1. Preheat your Hamilton Beach Breakfast Sandwich Maker until PREHEAT light gets green. 2. Lift the top cover, ring, and cooking plate. 3. Place half of the English muffin, cut-side up, inside the bottom tray of the sandwich maker. 4. Spread half of the fillings and place the other muffin half on top. 5. Now lower the cooking plate and top rings. 6. Cover the top hood, and let the sandwich cook for 5 minutes. 7. Rotate the handle of the cooking plate clockwise until it stops. 8. Lift the hood, the rings and transfer the sandwich to a plate. 9. Repeat the same steps with the remaining ingredients. 10. Serve.

Serving Suggestion: Serve the sandwich with a strawberry smoothie on the side.

Variation Tip: you can add some heavy cream to the filling as well.

Nutritional Information Per Serving: Calories 338 | Fat 7g |Sodium 316mg | Carbs 24g | Fiber 0.3g | Sugar 0.3g | Protein 3g

Chocolate Marshmallow Banana Sandwiches

Prep time: 15 minutes | Cook Time: 5 minutes | Serves: 2

Ingredients:

2 tablespoons unsalted butter
2 tablespoons dark brown sugar
4 slices buttermilk bread, cut into 4 inches round

8 whole large marshmallows
2 tablespoons semisweet chocolate chips
12 banana slices

Preparation:

1. Preheat your Hamilton Beach Breakfast Sandwich Maker until PREHEAT light gets green. 2. Lift the top cover, ring, and cooking plate. 3. Place a bread slice inside the bottom tray of the sandwich maker. 4. Spread ½ of the butter, sugar, chocolate chips, banana slices and marshmallows. 5. Now lower the cooking plate and top rings. 6. Place another bread slice on top. 7. Cover the top hood, and let the sandwich cook for 5 minutes. 8. Rotate the handle of the cooking plate clockwise until it stops. 9. Lift the hood, the rings and transfer the sandwich to a plate. 10. Repeat the same steps with the remaining ingredients. 11. Serve.

Serving Suggestion: Serve the sandwich with a mango smoothie on the side.

Variation Tip: you can add some whipped cream to the filling as well.

Nutritional Information Per Serving: Calories 110 | Fat 6g |Sodium 220mg | Carbs 32g | Fiber 2.4g | Sugar 1.2g | Protein 12g

Pumpkin Butter Chocolate Brie Sandwich

Prep time: 15 minutes | Cook Time: 5 minutes | Serves: 1

Ingredients:

2 slices of French bread, cut into 4 inches round
1 tablespoon butter softened
¼ cup pumpkin butter

2 ounces brie cheese sliced
1½ ounces chocolate broken into pieces

Preparation:

1. Preheat your Hamilton Beach Breakfast Sandwich Maker until PREHEAT light gets green. 2. Lift the top cover, ring, and cooking plate. 3. Place a bread slice inside the bottom tray of the sandwich maker. 4. Spread butter, pumpkin butter, brie cheese and chocolate on top. 5. Now lower the cooking plate and top rings then. 6. Place another bread slice on top. 7. Cover the top hood, and let the sandwich cook for 5 minutes. 8. Rotate the handle of the cooking plate clockwise until it stops. 9. Lift the hood, the rings and transfer the sandwich to a plate. 10. Serve.

Serving Suggestion: Serve the sandwich with an avocado smoothie on the side.

Variation Tip: you can add some mascarpone to the filling as well.

Nutritional Information Per Serving: Calories 301 | Fat 5g |Sodium 340mg | Carbs 17g | Fiber 1.2g | Sugar 1.3g | Protein 15.3g

Dark Chocolate Pomegranate Sandwich

Prep time: 15 minutes | Cook Time: 5 minutes | Serves: 2

Ingredients:

4 slices whole-grain crusty bread, cut into 4 inches round
2 tablespoons dairy-free butter
4 tablespoons almond butter

2 mini squares of dark chocolate
2-3 tablespoons pomegranate perils

Preparation:

1. Preheat your Hamilton Beach Breakfast Sandwich Maker until PREHEAT light gets green. 2. Lift the top cover, ring, and cooking plate. 3. Place a bread slice inside the bottom tray of the sandwich maker. 4. Spread ½ of the butter, almond butter, chocolate and pomegranate perils. 5. Now lower the cooking plate and top rings. 6. Place a bread slice on top. 7. Cover the top hood, and let the sandwich cook for 5 minutes. 8. Rotate the handle of the cooking plate clockwise until it stops. 9. Lift the hood, the rings and transfer the sandwich to a plate. 10. Repeat the same steps with the remaining ingredients. Serve.

Serving Suggestion: Serve the sandwich with a chocolate smoothie on the side.

Variation Tip: you can add whipped cream to the filling as well.

Nutritional Information Per Serving: Calories 248 | Fat 23g |Sodium 350mg | Carbs 18g | Fiber 6.3g | Sugar 1g | Protein 40.3g

Strawberry Marshmallow Panini

Prep Time: 15 minutes | Cook Time: 5 minutes | Serves: 4

Ingredients:

4 tablespoons Dulce de Leche
4 large croissants, cut in half
8 strawberries, sliced

8 large marshmallows, cut into 4 slices
Cooking spray

Preparation:

1. Preheat your Hamilton Beach Breakfast Sandwich Maker. 2. Lift the top cover, ring, and cooking plate. Use the cooking spray. 3. Place the lower half of a croissant in the sandwich maker and top it with ¼th of the Dulce de Leche. 4. Now lower the cooking plate and top rings, then add ¼th of the strawberries and marshmallows. 5. Place the other top half of the croissant on top. 6. Cover the top hood, and let the sandwich cook for 5 minutes. 7. When finished cooking, rotate the handle of the cooking plate clockwise until it stops. 8. Lift the hood, the rings and transfer the sandwich to a plate. 9. Repeat the same steps with the remaining ingredients. 10. Serve.

Serving Suggestion: Serve the sandwich with your favorite sauce on the side.

Variation Tip: You can add a drizzle of paprika on top of the filling as well.

Nutritional Information Per Serving: Calories 284 | Fat 7.9g |Sodium 704mg | Carbs 38.1g | Fiber 1.9g | Sugar 1.9g | Protein 14.8g

Cranberry Turkey-Bacon Panini

Prep Time: 15 minutes | Cook Time: 5 minutes | Serves: 1

Ingredients:

2 slices of thick bread, cut in 4-inch circle
1 tablespoon butter
a few slices of turkey
a few sage leaves

1 tablespoon of cranberry sauce
1-ounce goat cheese
2 slices cooked bacon
1 slice Muenster cheese

Preparation:

1. Preheat your Hamilton Beach Breakfast Sandwich Maker. 2. Lift the top cover, ring, and cooking plate. 3. Place a bread slice in the sandwich maker and top it with sauce. 4. Now lower the cooking plate and top rings, then add rest of the fillings. 5. Add the other circle of the bread on top. 6. Cover the top hood, and let the sandwich cook for 5 minutes. 7. When finished cooking, rotate the handle of the cooking plate clockwise until it stops. 8. Lift the hood, the rings and transfer the sandwich to a plate. 9. Serve.

Serving Suggestion: Serve the sandwich with coleslaw and your favorite sauce on the side.

Variation Tip: You can add a lettuce leave to the filling as well.

Nutritional Information Per Serving: Calories 180 | Fat 3.2g |Sodium 133mg | Carbs 32g | Fiber 1.1g | Sugar 1.8g | Protein 9g

Chicken Tomato Guacamole Panini

Prep Time: 15 minutes | Cook Time: 5 minutes | Serves: 1

Ingredients:

2 slices gluten-free bread, cut in 4-inch circle
½ avocado mashed
3 slices of tomato

2 slices or sprinkle of vegan cheese or cheese of choice
4 ounces grilled chicken breast
Salt and black pepper to taste

Preparation:

1. Preheat your Hamilton Beach Breakfast Sandwich Maker. 2. Lift the top cover, ring, and cooking plate. 3. Place a bread slice in the sandwich maker. 4. Now lower the cooking plate and top rings, then add chicken and rest of the ingredients on top. 5. Add the other circle of the bread on top. 6. Cover the top hood, and let the sandwich cook for 5 minutes. 7. When finished cooking, rotate the handle of the cooking plate clockwise until it stops. 8. Lift the hood, the rings and transfer the sandwich to a plate. 9. Serve.

Serving Suggestion: Serve the sandwich with your favorite sauce on the side.

Variation Tip: Add some additional dried herbs to the filling.

Nutritional Information Per Serving: C Calories 122 | Fat 1.8g |Sodium 794mg | Carbs 17g | Fiber 8.9g | Sugar 1.6g | Protein 14.9g

Balsamic Mato Panini

Prep Time: 15 minutes | Cook Time: 5 minutes | Serves: 1

Ingredients:

2 sourdough bread slices, cut in 4-inch circle
2 slices fresh mozzarella
½ Mato sliced
Handful of basil leaves

2 tablespoons olive oil
1 teaspoon balsamic vinegar
Salt and black pepper to taste

Preparation:

1. Preheat your Hamilton Beach Breakfast Sandwich Maker. 2. Lift the top cover, ring, and cooking plate. 3. Place a bread slice in the sandwich maker. 4. Now lower the cooking plate and top rings then add Mato, and rest of the fillings. 5. Add the other circle of the bread on top. 6. Cover the top hood, and let the sandwich cook for 5 minutes. 7. When finished cooking, rotate the handle of the cooking plate clockwise until it stops. 8. Lift the hood, the rings and transfer the sandwich to a plate. 9. Serve.

Serving Suggestion: Serve the sandwich with coleslaw and your favorite sauce on the side.

Variation Tip: You can add a layer of your favorite sauce to the filling as well.

Nutritional Information Per Serving: Calories 307 | Fat 8.6g |Sodium 510mg | Carbs 22.2g | Fiber 1.4g | Sugar 13g | Protein 33.6g

Chocolate Marshmallow Panini

Prep Time: 15 minutes | Cook Time: 5 minutes | Serves: 1

Ingredients:

2 white bread slices, cut in 4-inch circle
2 tablespoons chocolate

1 jumbo marshmallow toasted

Preparation:

1. Preheat your Hamilton Beach Breakfast Sandwich Maker. 2. Lift the top cover, ring, and cooking plate. 3. Place one circle of the bread in the sandwich maker. 4. Top it with Hershey chocolate spread. 5. Now lower the cooking plate and top rings, then spread marshmallows on top. 6. Add the other circle of the bread on top. 7. Cover the top hood, and let the sandwich cook for 5 minutes. 8. When finished cooking, rotate the handle of the cooking plate clockwise until it stops. 9. Lift the hood, the rings and transfer the sandwich to a plate. 10. Serve.

Serving Suggestion: Serve the sandwich with crispy bacon and your favorite sauce on the side.

Variation Tip: Add some additional ground black pepper to the filling.

Nutritional Information Per Serving: Calories 198 | Fat 14g |Sodium 272mg | Carbs 34g | Fiber 1g | Sugar 9.3g | Protein 1.3g

Chocolate Raspberry Cream Cheese Panini

Prep Time: 15 minutes | Cook Time: 5 minutes | Serves: 2

Ingredients:

4 slices Panera Bread, cut in 4-inch circle
4-ounce cream cheese softened

4 tablespoons raspberry jam
½ cup chocolate ganache

Preparation:

1. Preheat your Hamilton Beach Breakfast Sandwich Maker. 2. Lift the top cover, ring, and cooking plate. 3. Place one circle of the bread in the sandwich maker. 4. Top it with ½ of the chocolate ganache, jam and cream cheese. 5. Now lower the cooking plate and top rings. 6. Add the other circle of the bread on top. 7. Cover the top hood, and let the sandwich cook for 5 minutes. 8. When finished cooking, rotate the handle of the cooking plate clockwise until it stops. 9. Lift the hood, the rings and transfer the sandwich to a plate. 10. Repeat the same steps with the remaining ingredients. 11. Serve.

Serving Suggestion: Serve the sandwich with your favorite sauce on the side.

Variation Tip: Add some additional dried herbs to the filling.

Nutritional Information Per Serving: Calories 245 | Fat 14g |Sodium 122mg | Carbs 23.3g | Fiber 1.2g | Sugar 12g | Protein 4.3g

Dark Chocolate-Raspberry Sandwiches

Prep time: 15 minutes | Cook Time: 5 minutes | Serves: 4

Ingredients:

¼ cup seedless raspberry preserves
8 (¼-inch) slices Portuguese, cut into 4 inches' rounds
12 (53-ounce) packages dark chocolate squares

8 teaspoons butter
Coarse sea salt

Preparation:

1. Preheat your Hamilton Beach Breakfast Sandwich Maker until PREHEAT light gets green. 2. Lift the top cover, ring, and cooking plate. 3. Place a bread slice, inside the bottom tray of the sandwich maker. 4. Spread ¼ of the raspberry preserves, chocolate squares, and butter on top. 5. Now lower the cooking plate and top rings. 6. Place another bread slice on top. 7. Cover the top hood, and let the sandwich cook for 5 minutes. 8. Rotate the handle of the cooking plate clockwise until it stops. 9. Lift the hood, the rings and transfer the sandwich to a plate. 10. Repeat the same steps with the remaining ingredients. 11. Serve.

Serving Suggestion: Serve the sandwich with a banana smoothie on the side.

Variation Tip: you can add sprinkles to the filling as well.

Nutritional Information Per Serving: Calories 293 | Fat 3g |Sodium 510mg | Carbs 12g | Fiber 3g | Sugar 4g | Protein 4g

Kanafeh Pistachios Cheese Sandwich

Prep time: 15 minutes | Cook Time: 12 minutes | Serves: 2

Ingredients:

Sandwiches

¾ cup kanafeh

4 teaspoons melted ghee

1 drop orange food coloring

4 slices bread, cut into 4 inches round

Rose orange blossom simple syrup

½ cup granulated sugar

¼ cup water

1 squeeze of lemon juice

4 extra teaspoon of ghee

4 ounces mozzarella cheese, sliced

Chopped pistachios, for garnish

⅛ teaspoon rose water

⅛ teaspoon orange blossom water

Preparation:

1. Mix all the sugar syrup ingredients in a saucepan and cook for 5-7 minutes on low heat with occasional stirring. 2. Mix melted ghee with orange food coloring in a bowl. 3. Preheat your Hamilton Beach Breakfast Sandwich Maker until PREHEAT light gets green. 4. Lift the top cover, ring, and cooking plate. 5. Place a bread slice inside the bottom tray of the sandwich maker. 6. Spread ½ of the kanafeh, cheese, pistachios and sugar syrup on top. 7. Now lower the cooking plate and top rings. 8. Place another bread slice on top and brush it with ghee mixture. 9. Cover the top hood, and let the sandwich cook for 5 minutes. 10. Rotate the handle of the cooking plate clockwise until it stops. 11. Lift the hood, the rings and transfer the sandwich to a plate. 12. Repeat the same steps with the remaining ingredients. 13. Serve.

Serving Suggestion: Serve the sandwich with an apple smoothie on the side.

Variation Tip: you can add some extra cream to the filling as well.

Nutritional Information Per Serving: Calories 185 | Fat 8g |Sodium 146mg | Carbs 5g | Fiber 0.1g | Sugar 0.4g | Protein 1g

Chapter 9 Keto Sandwich Recipes

88   Chicken, Cauliflower & Cranberry Cheese Sandwich

88   Herbed Bacon and Egg Sandwich

89   Beef and Watercress Sandwich

89   Zucchini and Sausage Cheese Sandwich

89   Chicken and Avocado Cheese Panini

90   Caprese Pepperoni Sandwich

90   Spinach and Avocado Cheese Panini

90   Cucumber Mushroom Panini

91   Prosciutto-Ham Cheese Sandwich

91   Mozzarella Bacon Chaffle Sandwich

92   Turkey Sausage and Cheddar Sandwich

92   Shredded Turkey and Avocado Cheese Sandwich

93   Tofu and Ham Cheese Sandwich

93   Pulled Pork and Tomato Sandwich

94   Poppy Seeds and Ham Sliders

94   Avocado and Cauliflower Sandwiches

95   Delicious Curried Turkey Sandwich

95   Mayo Beef Patty Sandwich

96   Beef Steak and Cheddar Sandwich

96   Tasty BLT Cauliflower Sandwich

97   Herbed Cauliflower Cheese Sandwich

97   Cheesy Cauliflower and Pork Sandwich

98   Crab Melt Mushroom Sandwich

98   Avocado Chicken Cheese Sandwich

Chicken, Cauliflower & Cranberry Cheese Sandwich

Prep Time: 15 minutes | Cook Time: 5 minutes | Serves: 1

Ingredients:

1 cauliflower head, riced cooked
1 egg beaten
1½ cups cheddar cheese, grated
12 mozzarella Cheese, sliced
⅛ teaspoon dried sage
⅛ teaspoon dried oregano
1 dash teaspoon ground mustard seed
1 dash teaspoon dried thyme

Black pepper, to taste
Butter for greasing
Parsley for garnishing
2 teaspoons of mayonnaise
2 tablespoons of dried cranberries
1 cup of cooked chicken
1 teaspoon of chopped parsley

Preparation:

1. At 350 degrees F, preheat your oven. 2. Blend cauliflower with egg, dried herbs, spices and grated cheese in a blender until smooth. 3. Line a suitable baking sheet with parchment paper and divide the cauliflower mixture into 3-4-inches equal rounds onto the baking sheet. 4. Bake the cauliflower circles for 5 minutes per side. 5. Preheat your Hamilton Beach Breakfast Sandwich Maker. 6. Lift the top cover, ring, and cooking plate. 7. Place one circle of the cauliflower bread in the sandwich maker. 8. Top it with 1 mozzarella cheese slice. 9. Now lower the cooking plate and top rings then place the remaining fillings. 10. Add the other circle of the bread on top and brush it with butter. 11. Cover the top hood, and let the sandwich cook for 5 minutes. 12. When finished cooking, rotate the handle of the cooking plate clockwise until it stops. 13. Lift the hood, the rings and transfer the sandwich to a plate. 14. Garnish with parsley. 15. Serve.

Serving Suggestion: Serve the sandwich with your favorite sauce on the side.

Variation Tip: Add some additional dried herbs to the filling.

Nutritional Information Per Serving: Calories 159 | Fat 3g |Sodium 277mg | Carbs 9g | Fiber 1g | Sugar 9g | Protein 2g

Herbed Bacon and Egg Sandwich

Prep Time: 15 minutes | Cook Time: 5 minutes | Serves: 6

Ingredients:

1 head riced cauliflower cooked
1 egg beaten
1½ cups cheddar cheese, grated
12 mozzarella Cheese, slices
⅛ teaspoon dried sage
⅛ teaspoon dried oregano

1 egg
1 bacon slice, cooked
Ground black pepper
Dash teaspoon dried thyme
Butter for greasing
Fresh parsley for garnishing

Preparation:

1. At 350 degrees F, preheat your oven. 2. Blend cauliflower with egg, dried herbs, spices and grated cheese in a blender until smooth. 3. Line a suitable baking sheet with parchment paper and divide the cauliflower mixture into 3-4-inches equal rounds onto the baking sheet. 4. Bake the cauliflower circles for 5 minutes per side. 5. Preheat your Hamilton Beach Breakfast Sandwich Maker. 6. Lift the top cover, ring, and cooking plate. 7. Place one circle of the cauliflower bread in the sandwich maker. 8. Now lower the cooking plate and top rings then pour the egg mixture. 9. Add the bacon, cheese slice and other circle of the bread on top and brush it with butter. 10. Cover the top hood, and let the sandwich cook for 5 minutes. 11. When finished cooking, rotate the handle of the cooking plate clockwise until it stops. 12. Lift the hood, the rings and transfer the sandwich to a plate. 13. Repeat the same steps with the remaining ingredients. 14. Garnish with parsley. 15. Serve.

Serving Suggestion: Serve the sandwich with crispy bacon and your favorite sauce on the side.

Variation Tip: You can add a layer of your favorite sauce to the filling as well.

Nutritional Information Per Serving: Calories 217 | Fat 12g |Sodium 79mg | Carbs 8g | Fiber 1.1g | Sugar 18g | Protein 5g

Beef and Watercress Sandwich

Prep Time: 15 minutes | Cook Time: 9 minutes | Serves: 1

Ingredients:

2 large egg
¼ teaspoon fresh basil, chopped
¼ teaspoon fresh Italian parsley, chopped
black pepper, to taste

½ teaspoon grated lemon zest
Salt, to taste
6 ounces freshly sliced rare roast beef
1 cup watercress

Preparation:

1. Beat egg with basil, black pepper, salt and parsley in a small bowl. 2. Set a pan with two 4-inches metal rings in it. 3. Pour half of the prepared egg mixture into each ring and cook for 1-2 minutes per side. 4. Preheat your Hamilton Beach Breakfast Sandwich Maker. 5. Lift the top cover, ring, and cooking plate. 6. Place one half of the egg in the sandwich maker. 7. Now lower the cooking plate and top rings then add remaining fillings. 8. Place the other top half of the egg circle on top. 9. Cover the top hood, and let the sandwich cook for 5 minutes. 10. When finished cooking, rotate the handle of the cooking plate clockwise until it stops. 11. Lift the hood, the rings and transfer the sandwich to a plate. 12. Serve.

Serving Suggestion: Serve the sandwich with crispy bacon and your favorite sauce on the side.
Variation Tip: Add some additional dried herbs to the filling.
Nutritional Information Per Serving: Calories 203 | Fat 8.9g |Sodium 340mg | Carbs 7.2g | Fiber 1.2g | Sugar 11.3g | Protein 5.3g

Zucchini and Sausage Cheese Sandwich

Prep Time: 15 minutes | Cook Time: 9 minutes | Serves: 1

Ingredients:

2 large egg
¼ cup grated zucchini
¼ teaspoon fresh Italian parsley, chopped
Salt, to taste

black pepper, to taste
1 (1.2-ounces) cooked pork sausage patty
1 (0.5-ounces) slice Cheddar cheese

Preparation:

1. Beat egg with zucchini, black pepper, salt and parsley in a small bowl. 2. Set a pan with two 4-inches metal rings in it. 3. Pour half of the prepared egg mixture into each ring and cook for 1-2 minutes per side. 4. Preheat your Hamilton Beach Breakfast Sandwich Maker. 5. Lift the top cover, ring, and cooking plate. 6. Place one half of the egg in the sandwich maker. 7. Now lower the cooking plate and top rings then add sausage patty and cheddar cheese. 8. Place the other top half of the egg circle on top. 9. Cover the top hood, and let the sandwich cook for 5 minutes. 10. When finished cooking, rotate the handle of the cooking plate clockwise until it stops. 11. Lift the hood, the rings and transfer the sandwich to a plate. 12. Serve.

Serving Suggestion: Serve the sandwich with your favorite sauce on the side.
Variation Tip: You can add a drizzle of lemon juice on top of the filling as well.
Nutritional Information Per Serving: Calories 198 | Fat 14g |Sodium 272mg | Carbs 7g | Fiber 1g | Sugar 9.3g | Protein 1.3g

Chicken and Avocado Cheese Panini

Prep Time: 15 minutes | Cook Time: 5 minutes | Serves: 2

Ingredients:

½ cup almond flour
¼ cup whey protein isolate
1 teaspoon xanthan gum
½ teaspoons baking powder
½ cup egg whites

1 avocado, sliced
1 slice ham
1 chicken patty, cooked
1 cheese slices
1 slice tomatoes

Preparation:

1. Mix almond flour with protein, xanthan gum, baking powder and egg whites in a 4-inch ramekin. 2. Cook this bread batter in the microwave for 1-2 minutes the slice into 2 equal sized slices. 3. Preheat your Hamilton Beach Breakfast Sandwich Maker. 4. Lift the top cover, ring, and cooking plate. 5. Place the lower half of the bread in the sandwich maker. 6. Now lower the cooking plate and top rings, then place ½ of the fillings on top. 7. Add the other circle of the bread on top. 8. Cover the top hood, and let the sandwich cook for 5 minutes. 9. When finished cooking, rotate the handle of the cooking plate clockwise until it stops. 10. Lift the hood, the rings and transfer the sandwich to a plate. 11. Repeat the same steps with the remaining ingredients. 12. Serve.

Serving Suggestion: Serve the sandwich with crispy bacon and your favorite sauce on the side.
Variation Tip: You can add a lettuce leave to the filling as well.
Nutritional Information Per Serving: Calories 351 | Fat 19g |Sodium 412mg | Carbs 3g | Fiber 0.3g | Sugar 1g | Protein 23g

Caprese Pepperoni Sandwich

Prep Time: 15 minutes | Cook Time: 5 minutes | Serves: 2

Ingredients:

½ cup almond flour
¼ cup whey protein isolate
1 teaspoon xanthan gum
½ teaspoons baking powder

½ cup egg whites
1 pepperoni slice
1 mozzarella cheese slice
1 slice tomatoes

Preparation:

1. Mix almond flour with protein, xanthan gum, baking powder and egg whites in a 4-inch ramekin. 2. Cook this bread batter in the microwave for 1-2 minutes the slice into 2 equal sized slices. 3. Preheat your Hamilton Beach Breakfast Sandwich Maker. 4. Lift the top cover, ring, and cooking plate. 5. Place the lower half of the bread in the sandwich maker. 6. Now lower the cooking plate and top rings, then place ½ of the fillings on top. 7. Add the other circle of the bread on top. 8. Cover the top hood, and let the sandwich cook for 5 minutes. 9. When finished cooking, rotate the handle of the cooking plate clockwise until it stops. 10. Lift the hood, the rings and transfer the sandwich to a plate. 11. Repeat the same steps with the remaining ingredients. 12. Serve.
Serving Suggestion: Serve the sandwich with crispy bacon and your favorite sauce on the side.
Variation Tip: You can add a drizzle of lemon juice on top of the filling as well.
Nutritional Information Per Serving: Calories 354; Fat 7.9g; Sodium 704mg; Carbs 6g; Fiber 3.6g; Sugar 6g; Protein 18g

Spinach and Avocado Cheese Panini

Prep Time: 15 minutes | Cook Time: 5 minutes | Serves: 2

Ingredients:

½ cup almond flour
¼ cup whey protein isolate
1 teaspoon xanthan gum
½ teaspoons baking powder
½ cup egg whites

1 slice Colby jack cheese
6 leaves spinach
2 slices tomatoes
½ avocado sliced

Preparation:

1. Mix almond flour with protein, xanthan gum, baking powder and egg whites in a 4-inch ramekin. 2. Cook this bread batter in the microwave for 1-2 minutes the slice into 2 equal sized slices. 3. Preheat your Hamilton Beach Breakfast Sandwich Maker. 4. Lift the top cover, ring, and cooking plate. 5. Place the lower half of the bread in the sandwich maker. 6. Now lower the cooking plate and top rings then place ½ of the fillings on top. 7. Add the other circle of the bread on top. 8. Cover the top hood, and let the sandwich cook for 5 minutes. 9. When finished cooking, rotate the handle of the cooking plate clockwise until it stops. 10. Lift the hood, the rings and transfer the sandwich to a plate. 11. Repeat the same steps with the remaining ingredients. 12. Serve.
Serving Suggestion: Serve the sandwich with your favorite sauce on the side.
Variation Tip: Add some additional ground black pepper to the filling.
Nutritional Information Per Serving: Calories 248 | Fat 16g |Sodium 95mg | Carbs 8.4g | Fiber 0.3g | Sugar 10g | Protein 14.1g

Cucumber Mushroom Panini

Prep Time: 15 minutes | Cook Time: 5 minutes | Serves: 2

Ingredients:

4 Portobello mushroom caps, pressed
1 small seedless cucumber, sliced
4 ounces sliced black olives, drained
1 small onion, quartered

1 red bell pepper, chopped
1 green bell pepper, chopped
¼ cup Brianna›s Real French Vinaigrette Dressing

Preparation:

1. Mix all cucumber and all the veggies in a bowl with the dressing. 2. Preheat your Hamilton Beach Breakfast Sandwich Maker. 3. Lift the top cover, ring, and cooking plate. 4. Place one circle of the mushroom in the sandwich maker. 5. Top it with ½ of the veggie mixture. 6. Now lower the cooking plate and top rings. 7. Add the other circle of the mushroom on top. 8. Cover the top hood, and let the sandwich cook for 5 minutes. 9. When finished cooking, rotate the handle of the cooking plate clockwise until it stops. 10. Lift the hood, the rings and transfer the sandwich to a plate. 11. Repeat the same with the remaining ingredients. 12. Serve.
Serving Suggestion: Serve the sandwich with crispy bacon and your favorite sauce on the side.
Variation Tip: You can add a lettuce leave to the filling as well.
Nutritional Information Per Serving: Calories 395 | Fat 9.5g |Sodium 655mg | Carbs 3.4g | Fiber 0.4g | Sugar 0.4g | Protein 28.3g

Prosciutto-Ham Cheese Sandwich

Prep Time: 15 minutes | Cook Time: 7 minutes | Serves: 2

Ingredients:

½ cup almond flour
¼ cup whey protein isolate
1 teaspoon xanthan gum
½ teaspoons baking powder
½ cup egg whites

1 pepperoni slice
1 slice ham
1 slice prosciutto
1 cheese slices
1 slice tomatoes

Preparation:

1. Mix almond flour with protein, xanthan gum, baking powder and egg whites in a 4-inch ramekin. 2. Cook this bread batter in the microwave for 1-2 minutes the slice into 2 equal sized slices. 3. Preheat your Hamilton Beach Breakfast Sandwich Maker. 4. Lift the top cover, ring, and cooking plate. 5. Place the lower half of the bread in the sandwich maker. 6. Now lower the cooking plate and top rings then place ½ of the fillings on top. 7. Add the other circle of the bread on top. 8. Cover the top hood, and let the sandwich cook for 5 minutes. 9. When finished cooking, rotate the handle of the cooking plate clockwise until it stops. 10. Lift the hood, the rings and transfer the sandwich to a plate. 11. Repeat the same steps with the remaining ingredients. 12. Serve.

Serving Suggestion: Serve the sandwich with your favorite sauce on the side.

Variation Tip: Add some additional dried herbs to the filling.

Nutritional Information Per Serving: Calories 361 | Fat 16g |Sodium 515mg | Carbs 9.3g | Fiber 0.1g | Sugar 18.2g | Protein 33.3g

Mozzarella Bacon Chaffle Sandwich

Prep time: 15 minutes | Cook Time: 10 minutes | Serves: 1

Ingredients:

Chaffle bread
½ cup mozzarella shredded
1 egg
Sandwich
1 bacon slice, cooked
1 lettuce leaf

1 tablespoon green onion diced
½ teaspoon Italian seasoning

1 tomato slice
1 tablespoon mayo

Preparation:

1. Mix mozzarella cheese, egg, green onion and seasoning in a bowl. 2. Set a non-stick skillet over medium heat. 3. Drop ½ of the cheese mixture into the skillet, spread it into 4 inches round and cook for 2 minutes per side. 4. Make another chaffle and keep them aside. 5. Preheat your Hamilton Beach Breakfast Sandwich Maker until PREHEAT light gets green. 6. Lift the top cover, ring, and cooking plate. 7. Place a chaffle in the sandwich maker. 8. Spread mayo, tomato, lettuce and bacon on top. 9. Add the other circle of the chaffle on top. 10. Now lower the cooking plate and top rings. 11. Cover the top hood, and let the sandwich cook for 5 minutes. 12. Rotate the handle of the cooking plate clockwise until it stops. 13. Lift the hood, the rings and transfer the sandwich to a plate. 14. Serve.

Serving Suggestion: Serve the sandwich with your favorite keto salad on the side.

Variation Tip: Add some additional veggies to the filling.

Nutritional Information Per Serving: Calories 361 | Fat 16g |Sodium 515mg | Carbs 9.3g | Fiber 0.1g | Sugar 18.2g | Protein 33.3g

Turkey Sausage and Cheddar Sandwich

Prep Time: 15 minutes | Cook Time: 9 minutes | Serves: 1

Ingredients:

2 large egg
¼ teaspoon fresh basil, chopped
¼ teaspoon fresh Italian parsley, chopped
Salt, to taste

black pepper, to taste
1 (1.2-ounces) fully cooked turkey sausage patty
1 (0.5-ounces) slice cracker-cuts sharp Cheddar cheese

Preparation:

1. Beat egg with basil, black pepper, salt and parsley in a small bowl. 2. Set a pan with two 4-inches metal rings in it. 3. Pour half of the prepared egg mixture into each ring and cook for 1-2 minutes per side. 4. Preheat your Hamilton Beach Breakfast Sandwich Maker. 5. Lift the top cover, ring, and cooking plate. 6. Place one half of the egg in the sandwich maker. 7. Now lower the cooking plate and top rings then add sausage patty and cheddar cheese. 8. Place the other top half of the egg circle on top. 9. Cover the top hood, and let the sandwich cook for 5 minutes. 10. When finished cooking, rotate the handle of the cooking plate clockwise until it stops. 11. Lift the hood, the rings and transfer the sandwich to a plate. 12. Serve.

Serving Suggestion: Serve the sandwich with crispy bacon and your favorite sauce on the side.

Variation Tip: You can add a lettuce leave to the filling as well.

Nutritional Information Per Serving: Calories 245 | Fat 14g |Sodium 122mg | Carbs 8g | Fiber 1.2g | Sugar 12g | Protein 4.3g

Shredded Turkey and Avocado Cheese Sandwich

Prep time: 15 minutes | Cook Time: 7 minutes | Serves: 1

Ingredients:

½ cup almond flour
¼ cup whey protein isolate
1 teaspoon xanthan gum
½ teaspoon baking powder
½ cup egg whites

1½ tablespoons mayonnaise
1 slice aged cheddar cheese
2 bacon slices
¼ sliced avocado
1½ ounces roasted turkey, shredded

Preparation:

1. Mix almond flour with protein, xanthan gum, baking powder and egg whites in a 4-inch ramekin. 2. Cook this bread batter in the microwave for 1-2 minutes the slice into 2 equal-sized slices. 3. Preheat your Hamilton Beach Breakfast Sandwich Maker until PREHEAT light gets green. 4. Lift the top cover, ring, and cooking plate. 5. Place a bread slice in the sandwich maker. 6. Now lower the cooking plate and top rings then place turkey and other fillings on top. 7. Add the other circle of the bread on top. 8. Cover the top hood, and let the sandwich cook for 5 minutes. 9. Rotate the handle of the cooking plate clockwise until it stops. 10. Lift the hood, the rings and transfer the sandwich to a plate. 11. Serve.

Serving Suggestion: Serve the sandwich with your favorite keto dip on the side.

Variation Tip: Add some additional cream to the filling.

Nutritional Information Per Serving: Calories 361 | Fat 16g |Sodium 515mg | Carbs 9.3g | Fiber 0.1g | Sugar 18.2g | Protein 33.3g

Tofu and Ham Cheese Sandwich

Prep time: 15 minutes | Cook Time: 15 minutes | Serves: 1

Ingredients:

½ cup almond flour
¼ cup whey protein isolate
1 teaspoon xanthan gum
½ teaspoon baking powder

½ cup egg whites
2 tofu slices
1 slice ham
1 cheese slices

Preparation:

1. Set a non-stick pan on medium heat and sear the tofu slices for 3 minutes per side. 2. Mix almond flour with protein, xanthan gum, baking powder and egg whites in a 4-inch ramekin. 3. Cook this bread batter in the microwave for 1-2 minutes the slice into 2 equal-sized slices. 4. Preheat your Hamilton Beach Breakfast Sandwich Maker until PREHEAT light gets green. 5. Lift the top cover, ring, and cooking plate. 6. Place a bread slice in the sandwich maker. 7. Now lower the cooking plate and top rings then place tofu, ham and cheese on top. 8. Add the other circle of the bread on top. 9. Cover the top hood, and let the sandwich cook for 5 minutes. 10. Rotate the handle of the cooking plate clockwise until it stops. 11. Lift the hood, the rings and transfer the sandwich to a plate. 12. Serve.

Serving Suggestion: Serve the sandwich with your favorite keto sauce on the side.

Variation Tip: Add some additional dried herbs to the filling.

Nutritional Information Per Serving: Calories 361 | Fat 16g |Sodium 515mg | Carbs 9.3g | Fiber 0.1g | Sugar 18.2g | Protein 33.3g

Pulled Pork and Tomato Sandwich

Prep Time: 15 minutes | Cook Time: 5 minutes | Serves: 2

Ingredients:

½ cup almond flour
¼ cup whey protein isolate
1 teaspoon xanthan gum
½ teaspoons baking powder
½ cup egg whites

1 pepperoni slice
1 slice bacon
¼ cup pulled pork
1 cheese slices
1 slice tomatoes

Preparation:

1. Mix almond flour with protein, xanthan gum, baking powder and egg whites in a 4-inch ramekin. 2. Cook this bread batter in the microwave for 1-2 minutes the slice into 2 equal sized slices. 3. Preheat your Hamilton Beach Breakfast Sandwich Maker. 4. Lift the top cover, ring, and cooking plate. 5. Place the lower half of the bread in the sandwich maker. 6. Now lower the cooking plate and top rings then place ½ of the fillings on top. 7. Add the other circle of the bread on top. 8. Cover the top hood, and let the sandwich cook for 5 minutes. 9. When finished cooking, rotate the handle of the cooking plate clockwise until it stops. 10. Lift the hood, the rings and transfer the sandwich to a plate. 11. Repeat the same steps with the remaining ingredients. 12. Serve.

Serving Suggestion: Serve the sandwich with crispy bacon and your favorite sauce on the side.

Variation Tip: Add some additional ground black pepper to the filling.

Nutritional Information Per Serving: Calories 405 | Fat 22.7g |Sodium 227mg | Carbs 6.1g | Fiber 1.4g | Sugar 0.9g | Protein 45.2g

Poppy Seeds and Ham Sliders

Prep time: 15 minutes | Cook Time: 7 minutes | Serves: 1

Ingredients:

½ cup almond flour
1/4 cup whey protein isolate
1 teaspoon xanthan gum
½ teaspoon baking powder
½ cup egg whites
¼ lb. Swiss cheese

¼ lb. uncured deli ham
1 tablespoon minced white onion
2 tablespoons unsalted butter
¼ tablespoon yellow mustard
¼ tablespoon poppy seeds
¼ teaspoon Worcestershire sauce

Preparation:

1. Mix almond flour with protein, xanthan gum, baking powder and egg whites in a 4-inch ramekin. 2. Cook this bread batter in the microwave for 1-2 minutes the slice into 2 equal-sized slices. 3. Mix Worcestershire sauce, mustard, mustard and onion in a bowl. 4. Preheat your Hamilton Beach Breakfast Sandwich Maker until PREHEAT light gets green. 5. Lift the top cover, ring, and cooking plate. 6. Place a bread slice in the sandwich maker. 7. Now lower the cooking plate and top rings then place all the fillings on top. 8. Add the other circle of the bread on top. 9. Cover the top hood, and let the sandwich cook for 5 minutes. 10. Rotate the handle of the cooking plate clockwise until it stops. 11. Lift the hood, the rings and transfer the sandwich to a plate. 12. Serve.
Serving Suggestion: Serve the slider with your favorite keto sauce on the side.
Variation Tip: Add some additional dried herbs to the filling.
Nutritional Information Per Serving: Calories 361 | Fat 16g |Sodium 515mg | Carbs 9.3g | Fiber 0.1g | Sugar 18.2g | Protein 33.3g

Avocado and Cauliflower Sandwiches

Prep time: 15 minutes | Cook Time: 15 minutes | Serves: 2

Ingredients:

1 head cauliflower, cut into florets
2 eggs
2 tablespoons almond flour
1 tablespoon coconut flour
½ teaspoon garlic powder
¼ teaspoon fine sea salt
½ teaspoon poppy seeds

1 tablespoon sesame seeds
1 teaspoon dried minced garlic
1 tablespoon dried minced onion
½ teaspoon coarse sea salt
1 avocado, mashed
2 tablespoons mayonnaise
½ cup shredded cheddar

Preparation:

1. At 350 degrees F, preheat your oven. 2. Blend cauliflower with almond flour, coconut flour, eggs, garlic powder, sea salt, poppy seeds, garlic and onion in a food processor. 3. Line a suitable baking sheet with parchment paper and divide the cauliflower mixture into 3-4-inches equal rounds with a hole at the center onto the baking sheet and drizzle seeds on top. 4. Bake the cauliflower circles for 10 minutes until golden brown. 5. Preheat your Hamilton Beach Breakfast Sandwich Maker until PREHEAT light gets green. 6. Lift the top cover, ring, and cooking plate. 7. Split the baked bagels in half. 8. Place one half of a bagel in the sandwich maker. 9. Now lower the cooking plate and top rings then add ½ of cheddar, mayo and avocado. 10. Place the other top half of the bagel on top. 11. Cover the top hood, and let the sandwich cook for 5 minutes. 12. Rotate the handle of the cooking plate clockwise until it stops. 13. Lift the hood, the rings and transfer the sandwich to a plate. 14. Repeat the same steps with the remaining ingredients. 15. Serve.
Serving Suggestion: Serve the sandwich with favorite keto smoothie on the side.
Variation Tip: Add a layer of spicy mayo and pickled veggies for a change of taste.
Nutritional Information Per Serving: Calories 245 | Fat 14g |Sodium 122mg | Carbs 8g | Fiber 1.2g | Sugar 12g | Protein 4.3g

Delicious Curried Turkey Sandwich

Prep time: 15 minutes | Cook Time: 17 minutes | Serves: 1

Ingredients:

½ cup almond flour
¼ cup whey protein isolate
1 teaspoon xanthan gum
½ teaspoon baking powder
½ cup egg whites
4 ounces turkey mince

¼ red onion, grated
½ garlic clove, crushed
½ teaspoons madras curry powder
1 tablespoon chopped coriander
½ egg yolk
½ tablespoons sunflower oil

Preparation:

1. Mix almond flour with protein, xanthan gum, baking powder and egg whites in a 4-inch ramekin. 2. Cook this bread batter in the microwave for 1-2 minutes the slice into 2 equal-sized slices. 3. Blend turkey with red onion, garlic, curry powder, coriander, and egg yolk in a food processor for 1 minute. 4. Set a suitable skillet with olive oil over medium-high heat. 5. Make 1 patty out of the turkey mixture. 6. Sear the turkey patty in the oil for 5 minutes per side. 7. Preheat your Hamilton Beach Breakfast Sandwich Maker until PREHEAT light gets green. 8. Lift the top cover, ring, and cooking plate. 9. Place a bread slice, cut-side up, inside the bottom tray of the sandwich maker. 10. Now lower the cooking plate and top rings then place a patty. 11. Place the other top half of the bun on top. 12. Cover the top hood, and let the sandwich cook for 5 minutes. 13. Rotate the handle of the cooking plate clockwise until it stops. 14. Lift the hood, the rings and transfer the sandwich to a plate. 15. Repeat the same steps with the remaining ingredients. 16. Serve.

Serving Suggestion: Serve the sandwich with your favorite keto salad on the side.
Variation Tip: Add some additional cheese to the filling.
Nutritional Information Per Serving: Calories 361 | Fat 16g |Sodium 515mg | Carbs 9.3g | Fiber 0.1g | Sugar 18.2g | Protein 33.3g

Mayo Beef Patty Sandwich

Prep time: 15 minutes | Cook Time: 17 minutes | Serves: 1

Ingredients:

½ cup almond flour
¼ cup whey protein isolate
1 teaspoon xanthan gum
½ teaspoon baking powder
½ cup egg whites
¼ lb. ground beef
1 pinch salt

1 pinch ground black pepper
½ tablespoon butter
¼ onion, sliced
1 teaspoon mayonnaise
1 slices rye bread
1 slices sharp cheddar cheese

Preparation:

1. Mix almond flour with protein, xanthan gum, baking powder and egg whites in a 4-inch ramekin. 2. Cook this bread batter in the microwave for 1-2 minutes the slice into 2 equal-sized slices. 3. Mix beef with black pepper, salt, butter and onion in a food processor for 1 minute. 4. Make 1 patty out of this mixture. 5. Sear the patty in a skillet for 5 minutes per side. 6. Preheat your Hamilton Beach Breakfast Sandwich Maker until PREHEAT light gets green. 7. Lift the top cover, ring, and cooking plate. 8. Place one bread slice inside the bottom tray of the sandwich maker then spread 1 teaspoon mayonnaise on top. 9. Place a beef patty and a cheese slice on top of the mayo. 10. Now lower the cooking plate and top rings. 11. Place another bread slice on top. 12. Cover the top hood, and let the sandwich cook for 5 minutes. 13. Rotate the handle of the cooking plate clockwise until it stops. 14. Lift the hood, the rings and transfer the sandwich to a plate. 15. Serve.

Serving Suggestion: Serve the sandwich with your favorite keto dip on the side.
Variation Tip: Add some additional black pepper to the filling.
Nutritional Information Per Serving: Calories 361 | Fat 16g |Sodium 515mg | Carbs 9.3g | Fiber 0.1g | Sugar 18.2g | Protein 33.3g

Beef Steak and Cheddar Sandwich

Prep Time: 15 minutes | Cook Time: 9 minutes | Serves: 1

Ingredients:

2 large egg
¼ teaspoon fresh basil, chopped
¼ teaspoon fresh Italian parsley, chopped
Salt, to taste
black pepper, to taste

1 beef steak, cooked and sliced
1 tablespoon pesto
1 tomato slice
1 cheddar slice

Preparation:

1. Beat egg with basil, black pepper, salt and parsley in a small bowl. 2. Set a pan with two 4-inches metal rings in it. 3. Pour half of the prepared egg mixture into each rings and cook for 1-2 minutes per side. 4. Preheat your Hamilton Beach Breakfast Sandwich Maker. 5. Lift the top cover, ring, and cooking plate. 6. Place one half of the egg in the sandwich maker. 7. Now lower the cooking plate and top rings then add beef, pesto, cheese and tomato slice. 8. Place the other top half of the egg circle on top. 9. Cover the top hood, and let the sandwich cook for 5 minutes. 10. When finished cooking, rotate the handle of the cooking plate clockwise until it stops. 11. Lift the hood, the rings and transfer the sandwich to a plate. Serve.

Serving Suggestion: Serve the sandwich with crispy bacon and your favorite sauce on the side.
Variation Tip: Add some additional ground black pepper to the filling.
Nutritional Information Per Serving: Calories 153 | Fat 1g |Sodium 8mg | Carbs 6.6g | Fiber 0.8g | Sugar 56g | Protein 1g

Tasty BLT Cauliflower Sandwich

Prep time: 15 minutes | Cook Time: 15 minutes | Serves: 4

Ingredients:

1 small head cauliflower
3 tablespoons almond flour
1 tablespoon coconut flour
2 eggs
½ teaspoon garlic powder
½ teaspoon fine sea salt
¼ teaspoon baking powder

1 pinch of black pepper
2 teaspoons poppy seeds
8 slices thick-cut bacon, cooked
1 large ripe tomato, sliced
4 leaves crispy leaf lettuce
4 tablespoons mayo

Preparation:

1. At 350 degrees F, preheat your oven. 2. Blend cauliflower with almond flour, coconut flour, eggs, garlic powder, salt, baking powder and black pepper in a food processor. 3. Line a suitable baking sheet with parchment paper and divide the cauliflower mixture into 3-4-inches equal rounds onto the baking sheet and drizzle seeds on top. 4. Bake the cauliflower circles for 5 minutes per side. 5. Preheat your Hamilton Beach Breakfast Sandwich Maker until PREHEAT light gets green. 6. Lift the top cover, ring, and cooking plate. 7. Place one circle of the cauliflower bread in the sandwich maker. 8. Spread 1 tablespoon mayo, 1 lettuce leaf, 1 tomato slice and 2 bacon slices on top. 9. Now lower the cooking plate and top rings. 10. Add the other circle of the cauliflower bread on top. 11. Cover the top hood, and let the sandwich cook for 5 minutes. 12. Rotate the handle of the cooking plate clockwise until it stops. 13. Lift the hood, the rings and transfer the sandwich to a plate. 14. Repeat the same steps with the remaining ingredients. 15. Serve.

Serving Suggestion: Serve the sandwich with keto salad on the side.
Variation Tip: You can add a layer of your favorite keto sauce to the filling as well.
Nutritional Information Per Serving: Calories 217 | Fat 12g |Sodium 79mg | Carbs 8g | Fiber 1.1g | Sugar 18g | Protein 5g

Herbed Cauliflower Cheese Sandwich

Prep Time: 15 minutes | Cook Time: 5 minutes | Serves: 6

Ingredients:

1 head riced cauliflower cooked
1 egg, beaten
1½ cups cheddar cheese, grated
12 mozzarella Cheese, slices
⅛ teaspoon dried sage
⅛ teaspoon dried oregano

dash teaspoon ground mustard seed
dash teaspoon dried thyme
ground black pepper
butter for greasing
fresh parsley for garnishing

Preparation:

1. At 350 degrees F, preheat your oven. 2. Blend cauliflower with egg, dried thyme, spices and grated cheese in a blender until smooth. 3. Line a suitable baking sheet with parchment paper and divide the cauliflower mixture into 3-4-inches equal rounds onto the baking sheet. 4. Bake the cauliflower circles for 5 minutes per side. 5. Preheat your Hamilton Beach Breakfast Sandwich Maker. 6. Lift the top cover, ring, and cooking plate. 7. Place one circle of the cauliflower bread in the sandwich maker. 8. Top it with 1 mozzarella cheese slice. 9. Now lower the cooking plate and top rings. 10. Add the other circle of the bread on top and brush it with butter. 11. Cover the top hood, and let the sandwich cook for 5 minutes. 12. When finished cooking, rotate the handle of the cooking plate clockwise until it stops. 13. Lift the hood, the rings and transfer the sandwich to a plate. 14. Garnish with parsley. 15. Repeat the same steps with the remaining ingredients. 16. Serve.

Serving Suggestion: Serve the sandwich with coleslaw and your favorite sauce on the side.

Variation Tip: You can add a lettuce leave to the filling as well.

Nutritional Information Per Serving: Calories 301 | Fat 5g |Sodium 340mg | Carbs 4.7g | Fiber 1.2g | Sugar 1.3g | Protein 15.3g

Cheesy Cauliflower and Pork Sandwich

Prep Time: 15 minutes | Cook Time: 5 minutes | Serves: 6

Ingredients:

1 head riced cauliflower cooked
1 egg beaten
1½ cups cheddar cheese grated
12 mozzarella Cheese, slices
⅛ teaspoon dried sage
⅛ teaspoon dried oregano

dash teaspoon ground mustard seed
dash teaspoon dried thyme
ground black pepper
1 cup pulled barbecue pork
butter for greasing
fresh parsley for garnishing

Preparation:

1. At 350 degrees F, preheat your oven. 2. Blend cauliflower with egg, dried herbs, spices and grated cheese in a blender until smooth. 3. Line a suitable baking sheet with parchment paper and divide the cauliflower mixture into 3-4-inches equal rounds onto the baking sheet. 4. Bake the cauliflower circles for 5 minutes per side. 5. Preheat your Hamilton Beach Breakfast Sandwich Maker. 6. Lift the top cover, ring, and cooking plate. 7. Place one circle of the cauliflower bread in the sandwich maker and top it with pork. 8. Top it with 1 mozzarella cheese slice. 9. Now lower the cooking plate and top rings. 10. Add the other circle of the bread on top and brush it with butter. 11. Cover the top hood, and let the sandwich cook for 5 minutes. 12. When finished cooking, rotate the handle of the cooking plate clockwise until it stops. 13. Lift the hood, the rings and transfer the sandwich to a plate. 14. Repeat the same steps with the remaining ingredients. 15. Garnish with parsley. 16. Serve.

Serving Suggestion: Serve the sandwich with coleslaw and your favorite sauce on the side.

Variation Tip: You can add a lettuce leave to the filling as well.

Nutritional Information Per Serving: Ca Calories 195 | Fat 3g |Sodium 355mg | Carbs 7.7g | Fiber 1g | Sugar 25g | Protein 1g

Crab Melt Mushroom Sandwich

Prep time: 15 minutes | Cook Time: 5 minutes | Serves: 4

Ingredients:

4 large Portobello mushrooms cap, split in half
Spray coconut oil
Salt and pepper to taste
8 ounces lump crab meat
3 tablespoons mayonnaise
½ teaspoon Worcestershire sauce
½ teaspoon old bay seasoning

¼ teaspoon sea salt
Dash black pepper
Dash cayenne pepper
½ cup finely shredded cheddar cheese
1 tablespoon chopped parsley
4 green onions sliced

Preparation:

1. Mix crab meat with mayonnaise, Worcestershire sauce, old bay seasoning, black pepper, salt, cayenne pepper, parsley and onion. 2. Preheat your Hamilton Beach Breakfast Sandwich Maker until PREHEAT light gets green. 3. Lift the top cover, ring, and cooking plate. 4. Place one circle of the mushroom in the sandwich maker. 5. Top it with cheese and ¼ of the crab mixture. 6. Now lower the cooking plate and top rings. 7. Add the other circle of the mushroom on top. 8. Cover the top hood, and let the sandwich cook for 5 minutes. 9. Rotate the handle of the cooking plate clockwise until it stops. 10. Lift the hood, the rings and transfer the sandwich to a plate. 11. Repeat the same with the remaining ingredients. 12. Serve.

Serving Suggestion: Serve the sandwich with crispy bacon and your favorite keto sauce on the side.
Variation Tip: Add a layer of pickled onions for a change of taste.
Nutritional Information Per Serving: Calories 395 | Fat 9.5g |Sodium 655mg | Carbs 3.4g | Fiber 0.4g | Sugar 0.4g | Protein 28.3g

Avocado Chicken Cheese Sandwich

Prep Time: 15 minutes | Cook Time: 5 minutes | Serves: 2

Ingredients:

½ cup almond flour
¼ cup whey protein isolate
1 teaspoon xanthan gum
½ teaspoons baking powder
½ cup egg whites

½ avocado mashed
3 slices of tomato
2 slices cheese
4 ounces grilled chicken breast
Salt and black pepper to taste

Preparation:

1. Mix almond flour with protein, xanthan gum, baking powder and egg whites in a 4-inch ramekin. 2. Cook this bread batter in the microwave for 1-2 minutes the slice into 2 equal sized slices. 3. Preheat your Hamilton Beach Breakfast Sandwich Maker. 4. Lift the top cover, ring, and cooking plate. 5. Place the lower half of the bread in the sandwich maker. 6. Now lower the cooking plate and top rings then place ½ of the fillings on top. 7. Add the other circle of the bread on top. 8. Cover the top hood, and let the sandwich cook for 5 minutes. 9. When finished cooking, rotate the handle of the cooking plate clockwise until it stops. 10. Lift the hood, the rings and transfer the sandwich to a plate. 11. Repeat the same steps with the remaining ingredients. 12. Serve.

Serving Suggestion: Serve the sandwich with crispy bacon and your favorite sauce on the side.
Variation Tip: Add some additional dried herbs to the filling.
Nutritional Information Per Serving: Calories 361 | Fat 10g |Sodium 218mg | Carbs 6g | Fiber 10g | Sugar 30g | Protein 14g

Conclusion

With the Hamilton Beach Breakfast Sandwich Maker, the possibilities for delicious and customized breakfast sandwiches are endless. From classic combinations to more adventurous creations, this appliance makes it easy and convenient to enjoy a hot, fresh breakfast sandwich anytime you want. We hope that this book has provided you with the guidance you need to explore the full potential of the Hamilton Beach Breakfast Sandwich Maker. With its simple yet innovative design, this appliance is a game-changer for anyone who loves breakfast sandwiches. So go ahead, experiment with different ingredients and flavor combinations, and make the perfect breakfast sandwich that suits your taste buds. And always remember, with the Hamilton Beach Breakfast Sandwich Maker, a delicious breakfast sandwich is never more than a few minutes away!

Appendix 1 Measurement Conversion Chart

VOLUME EQUIVALENTS (LIQUID)

US STANDARD	US STANDARD (OUNCES)	METRIC (APPROXIMATE)
2 tablespoons	1 fl.oz	30 mL
¼ cup	2 fl.oz	60 mL
½ cup	4 fl.oz	120 mL
1 cup	8 fl.oz	240 mL
1½ cup	12 fl.oz	355 mL
2 cups or 1 pint	16 fl.oz	475 mL
4 cups or 1 quart	32 fl.oz	1 L
1 gallon	128 fl.oz	4 L

TEMPERATURES EQUIVALENTS

FAHRENHEIT (F)	CELSIUS (C) (APPROXIMATE)
225°F	107°C
250°F	120°C
275°F	135°C
300°F	150°C
325°F	160°C
350°F	180°C
375°F	190°C
400°F	205°C
425°F	220°C
450°F	235°C
475°F	245°C
500°F	260°C

VOLUME EQUIVALENTS (DRY)

US STANDARD	METRIC (APPROXIMATE)
⅛ teaspoon	0.5 mL
¼ teaspoon	1 mL
½ teaspoon	2 mL
¾ teaspoon	4 mL
1 teaspoon	5 mL
1 tablespoon	15 mL
¼ cup	59 mL
½ cup	118 mL
¾ cup	177 mL
1 cup	235 mL
2 cups	475 mL
3 cups	700 mL
4 cups	1 L

WEIGHT EQUIVALENTS

US STANDARD	METRIC (APPROXINATE)
1 ounce	28 g
2 ounces	57 g
5 ounces	142 g
10 ounces	284 g
15 ounces	425g
16 ounces (1 pound)	455 g
1.5 pounds	680 g
2 pounds	907g

Appendix 2 Recipes Index

A

Apple Nutella Sandwich 73
Apple Raisin Sandwich 72
Apple Sandwich 68
Apricot and Brie Croissant 69
Asparagus-Prosciutto Muffin Sandwich 30
Avocado and Cauliflower Sandwiches 94
Avocado and Egg Cheese Sandwich 65
Avocado Chicken Cheese Sandwich 98

B

Bacon and Egg Sandwich 12
Bacon and Pineapple Cheese Sandwich 21
Bacon-Avocado Cheese Sandwich 72
Balsamic Mato Panini 84
Banana Chocolate Chip Panini 80
Basil Chicken Pizza Burgers 50
Basil Tomato Cheese Sandwiches 61
BBQ Pork Sandwich 20
Beef and Giardiniera Sandwich 19
Beef and Veggie Sandwich 24
Beef and Watercress Sandwich 89
Beef Cabbage Burgers 22
Beef Cheeseburger 17
Beef Mushroom Sandwich 21
Beef Patty Melts 22
Beef Steak and Cheddar Sandwich 96
Black Bean and Brown Rice Beet Burgers 64
Black Bean and Tomato Burgers 66
Black Bean Potato Burgers 65
Blackened Salmon Sandwich 40
BLT Egg Sandwich 29
Blueberry and Pear Croissant 68
Blueberry Muffin Hand Pies 81
Breakfast Frittata Sandwich 11
Brie Cheese Chocolate Panini 81
Brie Cheese Raspberry Sandwiches 82
Brie Strawberry Muffin Sandwich 80
Broccoli and Cucumber Sandwich 62
Butter Egg and Cheese Bagel 34

C

Cajun Chicken Sandwich 48
Caprese Pepperoni Sandwich 90
Celery and Egg Salad Sandwich 31
Cheddar Apple Bacon Croissant 69
Cheddar Ham Muffin 13
Cheddar Sausage Biscuit Sandwich 14
Cheese Apple Cinnamon Raisin Sandwich 62
Cheese Apple Ham Panini 78
Cheese Apple Pie Panini 79
Cheese Chicken and Avocado Sandwich 49
Cheese Chicken Patty Sandwich 50
Cheese Egg & Beans Muffin Sandwich 31

Cheese Egg Buttermilk Biscuit Sandwich 29
Cheese Egg Sandwich 10
Cheese Ham Biscuit Sandwiches 12
Cheese Sausage Egg Muffin Sandwich 14
Cheese Spinach and Avocado Panini 81
Cheese Spinach and Egg Sandwich 32
Cheese Turkey and Sauerkraut Sandwich 52
Cheese Turkey Mushroom Burgers 57
Cheese Zucchini Sandwich 36
Cheese-Egg Biscuit 59
Cheesy Cauliflower and Pork Sandwich 97
Cheesy Egg, Avocado, and Bacon Sandwich 15
Chicken and Avocado Cheese Panini 89
Chicken and Broccoli Sandwich 52
Chicken and Red Cabbage Sandwich 53
Chicken Tomato Guacamole Panini 84
Chicken, Cauliflower & Cranberry Cheese Sandwich 88
Chicken, Green Chiles and Avocado Pita Sandwich 54
Chili Turkey and Cilantro Burgers 57
Chipotle Turkey-Avocado Sliders 55
Chocolate Marshmallow Banana Sandwiches 82
Chocolate Marshmallow Panini 85
Chocolate Raspberry Cream Cheese Panini 85
Chocolate-Hazelnut Banana Sandwich 74
Chorizo Avocado Sandwich 32
Cinnamon Apple Sandwich 76
Classic Bacon, Lettuce, and Tomato Sandwich 10
Corned Beef and Coleslaw Sandwiches 24
Corned Beef and Sauerkraut Cheese Sandwich 24
Crab Melt Mushroom Sandwich 98
Cranberry Turkey-Bacon Panini 84
Cream Cheese Egg Sandwich 14
Crispy Chicken Biscuits 16
Crispy Chicken Sandwich 20
Crispy Fish and Onion Sandwich 39
Crispy Seafood Burger 44
Crispy Shrimp Avocado Burgers 46
Cucumber Mushroom Panini 90
Cumin Black Bean Burgers 63

D

Dark Chocolate Cherry Sandwich 75
Dark Chocolate Pomegranate Sandwich 83
Dark Chocolate-Avocado Sandwich 70
Dark Chocolate-Raspberry Sandwiches 85
Delicious Curried Turkey Sandwich 95
Delicious Lobster Muffin Sandwiches 42
Delicious Peach Bran Sandwich 74
Dill Shrimp Sandwich 43

E

Egg and Cheese Bagel 60
Egg and Ham Whole-Grain Sandwich 15
Egg and Red Pepper Cheese Sandwich 33

Egg Salad Muffin Sandwich 35
Egg Whites and Mozzarella Cheese Muffin 34
Egg Whites Cheese Ciabatta Sandwich 60
Egg-and-Ham Sandwich with Hummus 35
Egg, Anchovy and Ham Hamburgers 36

F
Flavorful Beef and Cheddar Sandwich 26
Flavorful Spinach Sandwich 62
Fresh Strawberry English Muffin Pies 79
Fried Egg Cheese Sandwich 33
Fried Egg, Tomato and Avocado Sandwich 37

G
Garlic Chickpeas Burgers 65
Garlicky Tofu-Onion Burgers 61
Green Peas and Egg Sandwiches 33
Grilled Chicken and Black Bean Sandwich 48

H
Ham and Olive Sandwich 30
Ham and Salami Cheese Sandwich 59
Herbed Bacon and Egg Sandwich 88
Herbed Cauliflower Cheese Sandwich 97
Herbed Cheese Spinach Sandwiches 10
Herbed Chicken and Bacon Burgers 56
Herbed Onion and Egg Cheese Muffins 13
Herbed Turkey and Cranberry Burgers 56
Homemade Peanut Butter Banana Sandwich 75
Homemade Tuna Burgers 40
Honey Nuts Sandwich 68
Honey Pistachio Sandwich 70
Honey-Mustard Turkey Burgers 55

J
Japanese Egg Sandwich 29
Japanese Strawberry & Kiwi Sandwich 71

K
Kanafeh Pistachios Cheese Sandwich 86

L
Lemon Shrimp and Cod Burgers 41
Lemony Chicken Salad Sandwich 49
Lime Tuna Salad Sandwich 45

M
Mango-Peach Sandwiches 69
Maple Bacon French Toast Breakfast Sandwich 15
Marinara Parmesan Egg Muffin 30
Mayo Avocado and Vegetables Sandwich 17
Mayo Beef Patty Sandwich 95
Mayo Beef Sandwiches 19
Mayo Egg Sandwich 34
Mayo Pork Sandwich 21
Mayo Tuna Cheeseburgers 45
Mexican Beans & Fried Egg Sandwich 16
Mini Vanilla Cake 78
Mixed Fruit Sandwich 71
Mozzarella Bacon Chaffle Sandwich 91
Mushroom, Avocado and Red Pepper Burgers 63

N
Nutella Blueberry Sandwich 74
Nutella Cinnamon Quesadilla 82
Nutella Raspberry Cheese Sandwich 73
Nutella-Avocado Cheese Sandwich 73

P
Parmesan Spinach Sandwich 13

Poppy Seeds and Ham Sliders 94
Prosciutto-Ham Cheese Sandwich 91
Provolone Mushroom Cheese Sandwich 60
Pulled Pork and Tomato Sandwich 93
Pumpkin Butter Chocolate Brie Sandwich 83
Pumpkin-Apple Sandwich 71

R
Raspberry Brie Pancake Sandwich 59
Raspberry English Muffin Pies 80
Red Cabbage and Jackfruit Burger 64
Ricotta Cheese Nectarine Biscuit 72
Roasted Beef and Cheese Muffin Sandwich 25

S
Salmon and Carrot Sandwich 41
Salmon Burgers with Harissa Mayo & Cumber Relish 46
Salmon Patty Sandwiches 43
Sausage and Waffle Sandwich 12
Sausage Breading Pudding Sandwich 32
Scallop Corn Bacon Burgers 43
Shredded Turkey and Avocado Cheese Sandwich 92
Shrimp Salad Burgers 40
Simple Beef Patty Melt 26
Smoked Turkey and Cucumber Sandwich 54
Smoky Steak and Cheeses Sandwich 23
Spiced Beef Hamburgers 27
Spiced Beef Onion Sandwiches 25
Spicy Curried Turkey Burgers 53
Spicy Greens Cheddar Sandwich 27
Spicy Mayo Patty Melts 23
Spicy Mushroom Kale Sandwich 11
Spinach and Avocado Cheese Panini 90
Spinach and Chicken Mushroom Burgers 51
Spinach and Ham Sandwich 31
Strawberry Marshmallow Panini 83
Strawberry Nutella Sandwich 75
Sweet & Spicy Chicken Sandwich 52

T
Taleggio Cheese Ham Sandwich 78
Tartar Cod and Slaw Sandwiches 42
Tartar Cod-Cucumber Sandwich 39
Tasty BLT Cauliflower Sandwich 96
Tasty Cod Sandwich 39
Tasty Nutella Banana Panini 79
Tempeh Carrot Tomato Sandwich 66
Thai-Style Tuna & Cucumber Burgers 44
Tofu and Ham Cheese Sandwich 93
Tuna Olive Hamburgers 45
Turkey and Mushroom Sandwich 53
Turkey and Water Chestnut Burger 48
Turkey Sausage and Cheddar Sandwich 92
Turkey Tomato Burgers 50
Tzatziki Turkey Burgers 51

W
White Chocolate-Nut Sandwich 70

Y
Yogurt Chicken and Cheery Sandwich 49

Z
Zucchini and Sausage Cheese Sandwich 89

Made in the USA
Las Vegas, NV
29 November 2024

12939899R00062